Interest Groups, Lobbying, and Participation in America

Understanding why individuals participate in politics demands attention to more than just individual attributes and attitudes. Similarly, understanding how interest groups influence policy making demands attention to more than just the financial donations and direct activities of Washington-based lobbyists. To answer fundamental questions about what determines when and why people participate in politics and how organized interests go about trying to influence legislative decision making, we must understand how and why political leaders recruit which members of the public into the political arena. Looking from the bottom up with survey data and from the top down with data from interest group interviews, Kenneth Goldstein develops and tests a theory of how tactical choices in a grass roots campaign are made. In doing so, he demonstrates that outside lobbying activities deserve a place in any correctly specified model of interest group influence, political participation, or legislative decision making.

Kenneth M. Goldstein is assistant professor of political science at Arizona State University. He earned his Ph.D. in political science at the University of Michigan. His published work has appeared in the *American Journal of Political Science* and *Public Opinion Quarterly* and in a series of book chapters. He is currently at work on a project on television advertising. Goldstein has also had extensive professional experience in conducting survey research for media and political clients. He currently works as a consultant for the ABC News political unit.

Interest Groups, Lobbying, and Participation in America

KENNETH M. GOLDSTEIN
Arizona State University

148341

PUBLISHED BY THE PRESS SYNDICATE OF THE UNIVERSITY OF CAMBRIDGE
The Pitt Building, Trumpington Street, Cambridge, United Kingdom

CAMBRIDGE UNIVERSITY PRESS
The Edinburgh Building, Cambridge CB2 2RU, UK   www.cup.cam.ac.uk
40 West 20th Street, New York, NY 10011-4211, USA   www.cup.org
10 Stamford Road, Oakleigh, Melbourne 3166, Australia
Ruiz de Alarcón 13, 28014 Madrid, Spain

First published 1999

Printed in the United States of America

Typeface Plantin 10/12   *System* MagnaType™ [AG]

*A catalog record for this book is available from
the British Library.*

Library of Congress Cataloging in Publication data
Goldstein, Kenneth M., 1965–
Interest groups, lobbying, and participation in America / Kenneth
M. Goldstein.
p. cm.
Includes bibliographical references.
ISBN 0-521-63047-9. – ISBN 0-521-63962-X (pbk.)
1. Pressure groups – United States. 2. Lobbying – United States.
3. Political participation – United States. I. Title.
JK1118.G634 1999
324′.4′09732 – dc21   98-53581
                                                   CIP

ISBN 0 521 63047 9 hardback
ISBN 0 521 63962 X paperback

For Dan

Contents

List of Figures and Tables   *page* viii
Acknowledgments   xi

1   Introduction   1
2   Patterns and Puzzles in Participation and Lobbying   14
3   The Political Logic of Political Decisions   30
4   Explaining Lobbying Decisions   53
5   Lobbying Decisions and the Health Care Reform Battle   72
6   Patterns of Recruitment and Participation in the Mass Public   106
7   Conclusion   125

Appendix A: Sources and Coding for Survey Data   133
Appendix B: Interest Group Sampling Frame   138
Appendix C: Chronology of Health Care Reform Legislation   144

Bibliography   147
Index   153

Figures and Tables

Figures

2.1   Mail to House of Representatives, 1973–1994   *page* 16
2.2   Percentage of citizens contacting Congress to express
      opinion on issues, 1978–1994   17
2.3   Grass roots lobbying mentions in the press, 1977–1994   25
3.1   Major factors influencing congressional elections   32
3.2   Legislative decision making   37
6.1   Mobilization and participation in target and nontarget
      states   111

Tables

1.1   Issue areas and frequencies   7
1.2   Sample characteristics and response rates   9
3.1   Strategies for influencing congressional elections   35
3.2   Strategies to influence congressional decisions   42
3.3   Objectives, strategies, and legislative targets   48
4.1   Strategic objective by number of mobilization campaigns   55
4.2   Timing of mobilization campaigns with a legislative
      objective   59
4.3   Member targets with a legislative objective   60
4.4   Constituent mobilization targets with a legislative
      objective   62
4.5   Constituent mobilization targets with a legislative
      objective   64
4.6   Member targets with an electoral objective   68
4.7   Constituent mobilization targets with an electoral
      objective   69

4.8	Constituent mobilization targets with an electoral objective	70
5.1	Interviews by type of group	75
5.2	Where and when groups mobilized communications	78
5.3	Measures of committee competitiveness	80
5.4	Committee targets	81
5.5	Legislative targets within committee	84
5.6	Constituent mobilization targets and levels of leverage	87
5.7	Constituent mobilization targets	88
5.8	Handicapping House Energy and Commerce Committee	92
5.9	Member targets in House Energy and Commerce Committee	94
5.10	Handicapping House Ways and Means Committee	98
5.11	Member targets in House Ways and Means Committee	100
5.12	Handicapping Senate Finance Committee	102
5.13	Member targets in Senate Finance Committee	103
6.1	Targeted states	108
6.2	Personal characteristics and communicating with Congress on health care	110
6.3	Personal characteristics and being mobilized to contact Congress	112
6.4	Causes of phoning, faxing, or writing Congress on health care	113
6.5	Causes of being mobilized	114
6.6	Representation ratios for being mobilized	116
6.7	Targeted House districts	118
6.8	Individual characteristics and communicating to Congress	119
6.9	Causes of contacting Congress	120
6.10	Contacting Congress and partisanship	122
6.11	Proportion of Party identifiers and party voters by time of contact	122
6.12	Communicating with Congress to express opinion on issues, 1980–1994	123

Acknowledgments

As I finish this project, it's hard to know where to start the acknowledgments. I first owe a debt to the representatives of the many interest groups with whom I spoke. Without their time and openness, I would not have been able to complete this project. I would also like to thank the numerous journalists and consultants with whom I spoke.

I owe a great debt to my teachers and dissertation committee members at Michigan. Steve Rosenstone's advice and previous work were of great help in this project. Mayer Zald, from the sociology department, introduced me to a new literature and pushed me to think about my project from different angles. In fact, my dissertation grew out of a paper I wrote in his seminar on social movements. I thoroughly enjoyed the hours we talked about social movements, interest groups, and Michigan sports. Chris Achen and Greg Markus were also great teachers and friends. They both constantly pushed me to be rigorous in my theory and methods, but also understood my passion for politics and were fellow "political junkies." They gave early drafts careful reads. I enjoyed their insight and company tremendously during my time in Ann Arbor.

Although he was not on my committee, I would also like to thank John Kingdon. His research strategies and advice clearly influenced my work. Roy Pierce was a teacher and valued friend in Ann Arbor. Arlene Saxonhouse gave me the chance to teach a class in Washington, D.C., which gave me the opportunity to conduct the preliminary fieldwork for this project. Zvi and Marlene Gitelman treated me like family during my time in Ann Arbor.

In 1995 I was the recipient of a Gerald R. Ford Dissertation Fellowship. This award enabled me to conduct the large volume of interest group interviews. The Ford Fellowships are a tremendous resource that the department offers and I am very grateful.

Since I received help from so many people, I hesitate to single out one individual. I must note, however, the special influence Kent Jennings has had on my education over the past six years. From the class I took with Kent the first semester of my first year of graduate school to his work as cochair of my dissertation committee, he has been an inspirational teacher, mentor, role model, and friend. He is simply a class act, and I owe him a special debt of gratitude.

There are not words that can express my appreciation to my parents for all that they have done. They have provided love and support and I cannot thank them enough. Finally, I would like to thank my wife Amanda. She started this project as a girlfriend and she ends it as my wife and best friend. Her patience, love, and support – not to mention her careful editing – made this project possible.

1

Introduction

Grass roots 1. The common people.
2. The basic source or support.
Webster's New World Dictionary

Grass roots: The ultmate source of power, usually
patronized, occasionally feared.
Safire's Political Dictionary

In the summer of 1982, Senator Bob Dole, then chairman of the Senate Finance Committee, and Representative Dan Rostenkowski, then chairman of the House Ways and Means Committee, introduced legislation to withhold taxes on interest from bank accounts and dividends from securities. Proponents of the bill argued that most other types of income were already subject to withholding and that this legislation would simply plug a major tax loophole and tap a notorious source of unreported income. Arguments of this kind apparently convinced large majorities of both houses of Congress, and just before the August recess, the bill comfortably passed the Republican-controlled Senate and the Democrat-controlled House. The bill was signed by President Reagan and was scheduled to take effect within the year.

Fearful, however, of the multibillion-dollar cost of enforcing the law, the banking industry dropped "the hydrogen bomb of modern day lobbying, an effort whose firepower was awesome, whose carnage was staggering. In one fell swoop down went the chairman of the Senate Finance Committee, down went the chairman of the House Ways and Means Committee, down went the Secretary of the Treasury, down went the president of the United States" (Taylor 1983, A12). Led by the American Bankers Association (ABA) and the U.S. League of Savings, the banking industry used newspaper advertisements, posters in branches, and, most importantly, inserts in the monthly statements typically sent to all customers to encourage people to contact

1

Congress in opposition to the new law. The effort, orchestrated by the Chicago advertising and public relations firm of Leo Burnett and Company, deluged Congress with more than twenty-two million constituent communications (Berry 1989; Taylor 1983; Wittenberg and Wittenberg 1994; Wolpe 1990). Weeks later the House (382 to 41) and the Senate (94 to 5) reversed themselves and overwhelmingly repealed the withholding on interest and dividend income earned by individuals.

In a similar vein, Catastrophic Care legislation in 1989 began with wide bipartisan support and ended up being overwhelmingly repealed. The legislation was introduced as a way to protect elderly and disabled Americans from huge hospital and doctor bills. It resulted in a powerful Democratic committee chairman literally being chased through the halls of Congress by angry gangs of elderly constituents. Again, the goal of the legislation was to protect elderly and disabled Americans from astronomical medical bills. The mechanism to finance this benefit was a supplemental Medicare premium capped at $800. Although 40 percent of seniors would have been required to pay an extra premium, only about one in twenty elderly Americans would have had to pay the full capped amount (Wolpe 1990).

Groups like James Roosevelt's (FDR's oldest son) National Committee to Preserve Social Security and Medicare, however, opposed any increase in premiums no matter what the new benefits were. The group sent out mailings telling its five million members that the new law was a "seniors only tax" and suggested that all seniors would be forced to pay an extra tax for benefits that they already had. "Your Federal Taxes for 1989 may increase by up to $1,600 just because you are over the age of 65!" (Hosenball 1989). The claims of Roosevelt's group and other direct-mail organizations were half-truths at best. Still, millions of elderly Americans contacted their members of Congress and the bill was repealed less than a year later.

Now consider the dilemma of the "Big Three" automakers during the 1990 debate over the Clean-Air Act. *Newsweek* magazine (1991) described the challenge facing automobile companies: "How could they [the automakers] squash legislation that improved fuel efficiency, reduced air pollution and reduced dependence on foreign oil without looking like greedy corporate ghouls?" Jack Bonner, a prominent grass roots consultant, reasoned that smaller cars would hurt the elderly, the disabled, and those who must transport children.[1] So, in a matter of days, Bonner's "shock yuppies"

[1] Jack Bonner, president of Bonner & Associates, is probably the most well known grass roots consultant in Washington. In fact, it is nearly impossible to read a newspaper article or have a conversation about grass roots politics in Washington without Bonner's name popping up. Using more than two hundred articulate "unemployed policy junkies," Bonner's firm will scour congressional districts for groups and individuals to contact their representative from the grass roots in support of or in opposition to legislation of concern to his clients (Brinkley 1993b; Browning 1994; Gugliotta 1994). There is nothing particularly complicated about what Bonner does and he does not attempt to hide his efforts. He warns a Hill office when he

contacted elderly organizations, disabled groups, and the Boy Scouts in the constituencies of key conference committee members and created a torrent of opposition to higher fuel standards. In this way, Bonner helped change what easily could have been framed as an antienvironment vote into a pro-elderly, pro-disabled, and pro–Boy Scouts vote (*Newsweek* 1991).

In 1991, the American Bankers Association also turned to Bonner for help. In the fall of that year, the Senate had passed an amendment that would have regulated the interest rates banks could charge on credit cards. Because millions of Americans carried monthly balances on their credit card accounts, the bill looked like a winner. It was also one that would have taken a huge bite out of a major source of banking profits. In a four-day period, Bonner's firm was able to generate ten thousand phone calls from voters and community leaders in ten districts represented by members of the House Banking, Finance, and Urban Affairs Committee (Stone 1993, 755). When all was said and done, the amendment was not included in the House version of the bill and was subsequently dropped in a House and Senate conference committee.

The preceding cases provide prominent examples of what political scientists categorize as outside lobbying and what is known on Capitol Hill and in the professional community as grass roots lobbying or issue advocacy campaigns. Although there is no real formal definition of the tactic, popular and scholarly accounts alike consider grass roots or outside lobbying to be any type of action that attempts to influence inside-the-beltway inhabitants by influencing the attitudes or behavior of outside-the-beltway inhabitants. It stands in contrast to "inside strategies" such as private meetings with members and staff, testifying at committee hearings, and contributing money.

Grass roots lobbying is akin to the "going public" strategy "whereby a president promotes himself and his policies in Washington by appealing to the American public for support" (Kernell 1993, 2). Perhaps the best definition comes from a trade association executive speaking at a workshop on grass roots lobbying. He defined grass roots lobbying as "The identification, recruitment, and mobilization of constituent-based political strength capable of influencing political decisions."

Although it is tempting to make judgments about the effect of such interest group tactics, my goal in presenting these four examples was not to prove that grass roots lobbying was the decisive factor in the legislative battles. The four were complicated issues, and there are multiple explanations for the eventual outcomes in each case. For example, the Clean Air Act had been debated for years (Cohen 1992), and a stock market drop and the comments

is about to mobilize citizens in its district so that it can allocate staff time in advance to process the incoming faxes, letters, and phone calls. In fact, Bonner is even known to send flowers and chocolates to Hill receptionists the day before his efforts hit.

of legions of financial experts preceded the deletion of caps on credit card interest in the final banking bill (Knight 1991). Besides, in many other instances grass roots lobbying had no apparent effect.

These four cases do, however, illustrate how grass roots lobbying can be an effective tool for lobbyists to convey information. More specifically, these cases illustrate how grass roots lobbying can signal legislators on the electoral consequences of their actions and provide information to constituents that may reframe an issue and possibly change mass opinion. These four cases suggest that understanding why and how lobbying choices are made is a crucial first step toward understanding both the character of mass participation and the nature of interest group influence. With our current level of understanding, the appropriate question is not whether orchestrated communications have no effect (as many political scientists have assumed) or whether they decide every issue (as many journalists have assumed), but instead, why and how they are used? At the very least, these cases – and the recent explosion in participation and mobilization that I will describe in the next chapter – strongly suggest that there is probable cause to investigate when, where, why, and how interest groups go public.

The Argument

Cases such as the ones just described, as well as the apparent growth in both communications to Congress and the use of grass roots campaigns as a lobbying tactic, were the inspiration for this book. Yet my brief description of these four grass roots campaigns, which attempted to stimulate constituent communications, really provide no startling new information and would not surprise scholarly observers of interest groups or mass participation. After all, scholars of participation are well aware of the impact of elite behavior in stimulating various types of mass participation (Rosenstone and Hansen 1993; Verba, Schlozman, and Brady 1995a). Likewise, students of lobbying are well aware that outside tactics such as stimulating constituent communications to Congress are an important weapon in an interest group's arsenal of tactics (Schlozman and Tierney 1986).

The central argument made in this book is that the elite stimulus of mass participation binds together crucial questions of group influence and individual participation: When and why do people participate in politics? How do organized interests decide when, where, and how to influence public policy? These questions about mass participation and group influence, usually tackled separately by political scientists, strike at the heart of arguments about the state of democracy in America. To answer these two fundamental questions – to understand what determines when and why people participate in politics and how organized interests go about trying to influence legislative decision making – we must understand how and why political leaders recruit which members of the public into the political arena.

My goal is to develop and test a theory of how tactical choices in a grass roots campaign are made. My goal is to develop and test a theory of how tactical choices about when to lobby, where to lobby, and whom to lobby are made. In doing so, I demonstrate that outside lobbying activities deserve a place in any correctly specified model of interest group influence, political participation, or legislative decision making. Put another way, an understanding of why individuals participate in politics demands attention to more than just individual attributes and attitudes; and an understanding of how interest groups influence policy making demands attention to more than just the financial donations and direct activities of Washington-based lobbyists.

Yet, understanding how and why lobbying choices are made is difficult if we do not have an accurate theoretical picture of the strategic logic governing the use of grass roots lobbying. Although scholars have painted a more detailed theoretical and empirical picture of interest group formation and behavior in the past decade, the motives and goals of lobbyists are still not thoroughly understood. In fact, not knowing where to look may be one of the primary reasons why scholars have found it difficult to demonstrate interest group influence. For example, one of the problems with previous work on interest groups and lobbying has been that scholars have tried to identify the direct independent influence of particular strategies and tactics. A typical question is, With all else held constant, what is the independent direct influence of a PAC donation on a roll call vote? As these cases suggest, however, lobbyists may work indirectly through constituents to influence congressional decisions. A more detailed understanding of the strategic objectives of lobbying is required.

Similarly, in the mass participation literature, attention to the effects or goals of citizen activity is often divorced from attention to the causes or correlates of citizen activity. Indeed, the standard style in many studies of participation is to stipulate that participation matters and then to identify its causes. I contend that who participates and how participation matters are questions that should not be studied separately. It is not possible to understand elite efforts to stimulate mass participation and communications to Congress without also understanding the politics and political context in which grass roots lobbying and communications to Congress take place.

Data and Methodology

This book reports on empirical research designed to understand how and why interest groups utilize outside lobbying tactics. Although this study is primarily concerned with why and how interest groups decide which citizens to recruit into the political arena, I also discuss a broader range of tactics that interest groups use when they go public. To investigate the strategic calculations and decisions made by organized interests in such grass roots or outside lobbying campaigns, I utilize multiple sources of data collected in different ways and at different times.

One set of data utilized in this book consists of public opinion surveys. During the summer of 1994, I was able to add participation and recruitment questions to the Battleground Poll, a national survey jointly conducted by a Democratic polling firm and a Republican polling firm.[2] Although many surveys contain "contact Congress" questions and many surveys contain an "electoral mobilization" question, few studies specifically ask whether a respondent was recruited to lobby Congress and with respect to what issue. Data from the Battleground Poll enable me to test specifically the effect of recruitment contacts on individuals and to investigate who, in fact, is being recruited.

In addition, a large-sample Times-Mirror survey conducted in July 1994 provides another barometer of citizen participation during the identical time period and also affords another opportunity to investigate the effect of targeted districts on political participation. I also use data from the National Election Studies (NES) in this book. The NES data provide a time series on participation, permitting me to analyze how the quantity and partisan composition of those who contact Congress have changed over time.

These data sources are certainly valuable for my purposes. Nevertheless, to understand grass roots lobbying and mass participation, it is vital to go beyond the sample survey. Accordingly, the main body of research in this book comes from data gathered in forty-one in-depth personal interviews with interest group representatives.[3] The unit of analysis, however, is neither the individual whom I interviewed nor the group he or she represented. It is instead the individual grass roots lobbying campaigns and tactical choices that were made. In most of the interviews, more than one lobbying campaign and more than one set of tactical choices were discussed. Altogether, the forty-one interviews covered ninety-four separate grass roots lobbying campaigns across fifteen issue domains. Table 1.1 lists the issues discussed and their frequency of occurrence.

---

[2] Thanks to Celinda Lake, now of Lake Research, Ed Goeas of The Tarrance Group, and Lori Gudermuth, now of Public Opinion Strategies, for allowing me to insert recruitment and participation questions in the Battleground Poll.

[3] I did not enjoy a good response from a pretest of interest groups that I conducted by mail. On the other hand, in pretest interviews that I conducted in person, I was able to gather both information about specific mobilization decisions as well as in-depth background information on how grass roots mobilization tactics were utilized.

Table 1.1. *Issue Areas and Frequencies*

Issue	Number of Mobilization Efforts Examined
Health Care	21
Clinton Budget/Stimulus Package	12
NAFTA	12
Medicare *	10
Crime Bill/Assault Weapons	8
Balanced Budget Amendment	6
Federal Funding Abortion	5
Tort Reform *	4
Term Limits *	4
Telecommunications *	4
Campaign Finance	2
Lobbying Reform	2
Smoking/Tobacco	2
Worker Safety *	1
Meat Inspections *	1
Total	94

* 104th Congress.
Source: Author's interviews.

The forty-one interviews come from a sample of eighty organizations that were drawn from a list I compiled of 191 interest groups pursuing grass roots tactics in the 103rd Congress. Compiling such a sampling frame was not a straightforward task. Although there are many lists of interest groups and lobbyists available (*Washington Representatives* is probably the most extensive), there is no roster of groups that specifically employ the tactic of stimulating constituent communications to Congress. In fact, the lobbying reform bill that was finally passed in 1995 specifically excluded requiring groups to register if they stimulate constituent communications. Furthermore, many groups employ consultants and other third parties to conduct their grass roots campaigns. So, with no readily available list from which to sample, I created a sampling frame from different media and political sources.

First, from April through November 1994, while working in Washington, I monitored on a daily basis the *New York Times,* the *Wall Street Journal,* and the *Washington Post,* making note of any ideological group, union, trade association, or corporation that was mentioned as pursuing grass roots tactics. Second, I also monitored two weekly publications that cover Congress, interest groups, and professional activity inside the beltway: *Congressional Quarterly Weekly Report* and the *National Journal.* Third, I monitored the *Hotline,* a daily briefing memo of political news that summarizes reports from media outlets from all over the country, and the *Healthline,* a similar service that concentrates solely on the policy and politics surrounding health care legislation.[4] Fourth, I obtained a copy of the registration list for the Public Affairs Council's annual workshop on mobilization tactics. (See Appendix B for a list of the groups in the sampling frame.)

Using the list derived from these sources, I drew a random sample of twenty groups from each of the four different types of interest groups and sent letters requesting confidential, not-for-direct-attribution interviews to representatives of eighty groups.[5] In the case of unions and left-leaning ideological groups, the initial response to my letters was quite poor.[6] Therefore, I used the introductions of friends in Washington to gain access to two of these groups and then used these connections to schedule other interviews.[7] Even with this snowball method, the interviews were with groups that were originally on my list. All told, I received responses from forty-eight groups and eventually interviewed representatives from forty-one for a response rate of 51 percent. Table 1.2 shows the distribution of groups in my sampling frame and final sample, as well as response rates and the number of grass roots campaigns discussed.[8]

Since the unit of analysis was individual lobbying campaigns, there was an added level of sampling. My first question to the interest group representatives I interviewed was to name three recent issues in which they employed grass roots tactics. Even though my goal was to talk about all the recent issues where a group pursued a grass roots strategy that attempted to stimu-

---

[4] While the monitoring of all these publications obviously could have been done anywhere, working in an office that had each of these papers and magazines delivered made the process much easier.

[5] The interview requests were sent on University of Michigan Department of Political Science stationery, and I identified myself as a graduate student conducting dissertation research.

[6] This experience is similar to reports I have heard from other scholars. It is also similar to Jack Walker's experience with his mail survey of interest groups, where unions had the lowest response rate and were not used in his analysis (1991).

[7] In general, I also found that unions and ideological groups were not as forthcoming in the interviews. They allowed me to look at fewer background documents and gave me less detailed behind-the-scenes explanations. In a significant finding for future social science research methods, the one exception to this rule was the union representative whom I interviewed at a bar!

[8] A recent mass survey of interest groups yielded the following distribution of interest group types (Leech 1997): trade associations, 28 percent; professional associations, 20 percent; businesses and corporations, 19 percent; government and institutions, 5 percent; and other nonprofits, 28 percent.

Table 1.2. *Sample Characteristics and Response Rates*

Group Type	Number in Sampling Frame	Interviews Requested	Completed Interviews	Mobilization Campaigns
Trade Associations	54	20	10	23
Corporations	55	20	11	16
Citizens' Groups	56	20	12	37
Labor Unions	26	20	8	18
Total	191	80	41	94

Note: In his 1985 survey of interest groups Walker used the *Washington Information Directory*, published by Congressional Quarterly Press, for his sampling frame. Because Walker was primarily interested in how organizational factors influence strategies, he excluded corporations from his sample. For-profit trade associations composed 37.8 percent of his sample, not-for-profit trade associations composed 32.5 percent, mixed-trade associations composed 5.8 percent, and citizen groups composed 23.9 percent (Walker 1991, 51).

late constituent communications, time often did not permit this. This sampling method focused on the first campaign that a respondent picked and likely yielded larger and more prominent campaigns.[9]

The research strategy of discussing specific issues differs from how some scholars have previously studied interest group tactics and tactical decisions. Most previous surveys of interest groups have asked respondents to generalize about their activities and the rationale behind their actions (Berry 1977; Schlozman and Tierney 1986; Walker 1991). Although these surveys provided extraordinarily valuable information, their methods make it impossible to understand the political context or political environment in which lobbying decisions take place. Wanting to understand how the political environment influences political decisions and believing that respondents would be best able to describe their actual choices, my method borrows from Kingdon (1989). Specifically, I asked my informants to talk about their decision making in the context of particular political issues.[10]

The great majority of the interviews were conducted in person in the Washington, D.C. offices of the selected groups. Most of the interviews were completed between February and November 1995. Three of the interviews, however, were conducted at corporate headquarters outside the beltway; three were conducted on the phone; one was conducted in a taxi as I accompanied one of my respondents on a trip to Dulles Airport; and one was conducted at a bar.

The interest group representatives with whom I spoke were familiar with the rules for not-for-attribution interviews and seemed comfortable with my note taking. Occasionally – usually after a particularly frank comment – informants would remind me that their comments were not-for-attribution. During the interview I coded responses to questions from my interview schedule about strategic objectives as well as constituent and legislator targeting. In only a few cases did I have to push a respondent to explain to me more clearly his or her organization's strategic goal or tactical choices on a particular lobbying campaign. (See Appendix B for the interview instrument.)

Although my goal was to gather basic quantifiable information about the maximum number of lobbying choices, I also wanted to give respondents the opportunity to provide me with more in-depth information and a greater understanding of how grass roots lobbying campaigns are conducted. In other words, while still striving to gather basic information from every inter-

---

[9] If I were to carry out a similar study in the future, I would choose a random number before starting the interview and begin my interview with the "nth" issue mentioned in response to my first question. This would minimize the focus on the first (and most prominent) campaign that a respondent decided to discuss.

[10] A similar strategy was followed by Browne (1988, 1995), and Hansen (1991).

view, I also wanted to take advantage of the access I had gained and the knowledge and inside insights of my informants. Therefore, if I was getting particularly frank, colorful, or more in-depth information, I would not hesitate to deviate from the interview schedule.

To reiterate, the list from which I drew my sample was not an exhaustive and unbiased one of groups pursuing grass roots tactics. Therefore, the interview data do not reflect a random sample of all interest groups that orchestrated constituent communications, nor all tactical decisions that were made around issues in the 103rd and 104th Congresses.[11] Although it is impossible to measure bias with no information on exactly what the population should look like, my sample drawn from media sources surely overrepresents large, prominent, and media-friendly groups. Consequently, it is impossible to make inferences about all groups, all mobilization campaigns, or all tactical choices from the frequencies in my data. What's more, the data do not permit judgments to be made about the effectiveness of grass roots mobilization as a lobbying tactic.

Nevertheless, whereas in a perfect world a random sample of groups pursuing grass roots tactics would have been readily available, the goal of this research was not to measure the effect, frequency, or even organizational factors that allow grass roots campaigns to be pursued. Instead, the goal of this research was to study strategic calculations and political decision making. Although no claim is made that they perfectly represent the entire universe of groups pursuing grass roots mobilization strategies, I sampled and completed interviews with a wide range of groups holding diverse ideologies, goals, and organizational structures. All in all, the data from these interviews provided a substantial first step toward understanding how and why interest groups stimulate the grass roots.

Taking a page from Richard Fenno (1978), many of the arguments made in this book are also informed by a significant amount of soaking and poking. For instance, over an eight-month period during 1994, I worked as a participant-observer pollster with a political consulting firm in Washington, D.C. This experience provided me with a unique vantage point from which to view electoral and legislative politics preceding the 1994 election. The firm's client list not only included many Democratic congressional candidates, but scores of interest groups on both sides of every imaginable fence.[12] My experience working in Washington allowed me to immerse

---

[11] Although my sampling frame was comprised of groups pursuing grass roots strategies in the 103rd Congress, many of these groups also pursued similar tactics in the 104th Congress. Therefore, my sample of grass roots campaigns also includes issues from the 104th Congress.

[12] From May to November of 1994 I worked as a senior analyst for the Washington, D.C., polling firm of Mellman-Lazarus-Lake. Its client list included four incumbent Democrats

myself in the political process – to observe and talk with members of Congress, interest group representatives, and congressional and White House staff, as well as other consultants. In addition, I drew on information gathered at workshops for grass roots professionals and my own experiences and observations as a journalist to understand the strategies and tactics as well as the methods and technologies involved in stimulating constituent communications to Congress.

Plan of the Book

In Chapter 2, I trace the rise of communications to Congress and briefly discuss some previous work on lobbying and participation. I discuss how the traditional explanations for participation have a difficult time accounting for differences in rates of communication to Congress from year to year and district to district (not to mention why any citizens contact Congress at all). Although mobilization by elites appears to be a possible solution and is on the rise as a lobbying tactic, I also discuss how traditional explanations of lobbying tell us little about when, where, and toward whom is the tactic likely to be used.

In Chapter 3, I draw on the participation, legislative behavior, and interest group literatures to devise a theoretical model to understand why and how strategic and grass roots lobbying decisions are made. I argue that lobbyists have varied motives and that their tactical choices depend on their strategic objectives and the information they must convey to legislators and constituents. I argue that targeting decisions are a multistage process in which lobbyists attempt to evaluate the influence that a particular individual's communication to Congress will have on the eventual outcome of a particular legislative or electoral fight. These tactical judgments ultimately determine decisions about when to target, where to target, whom to target, and how to target. In building a theory, I argue that these judgments are based on the fact that, unlike votes in an election, communications to Congress are not interchangeable. More precisely, I argue that the effect of a communication on the policy process is a function of the individual com-

who lost their bids for reelection: Speaker Tom Foley (Washington), Rep. Jolene Unsoeld (Washington), Rep. David Price (North Carolina), and Rep. Larry LaRocco (Idaho), as well as the House Democratic Caucus. In addition, two Democratic incumbents who won by only a few thousand votes, Rep. Sander Levin (Michigan) and Rep. Elizabeth Furse (Oregon), were also clients. While this was unfortunate for the firm, it provided an excellent vantage point from which to witness the forces that defeated Democratic incumbents in 1994. The firm's client list also included current House Minority Leader Dick Gephardt (Missouri) and Senate Minority Leader Tom Daschle (South Dakota). Interest group clients included COPE, Human Rights Campaign Fund, and the League of Conservation Voters. Corporate clients included chemical giant Freeport McMoran and the five largest insurance companies.

municating, the legislator being communicated to, and the message needing to be communicated.

In Chapter 4, I begin the empirical tests of my theory of grass roots lobbying choices. I use data gathered from seventy-three grass roots lobbying campaigns to examine when, where, and how groups recruit citizens into politics, and who gets recruited. In addition to the interviews, I reviewed primary documents and media accounts and made use of my own experiences as a journalist and political consultant.

Chapter 5 turns to the specific case of health care. The debate over health care reform and the Clinton plan, which would have changed the way one-seventh of the economy functions, was one of the biggest policy battles in recent memory. Using a combination of media accounts, professional publications, and interviews with many of the major policy and lobbying players, I examine the role elite-orchestrated mass participation played in the battle over health care reform. I use this case as a way to test the assumptions from the theoretical framework as well as a way to acquire information about legislative and citizen targets during the summer of 1994. Such information about targeted states and districts is critical in testing a strategic model of mobilization and how participation between elections works.

In Chapter 6, I utilize the two sets of survey data – a 1994 Battleground Poll and a 1994 Times-Mirror poll – to explore patterns of lobbying and participation. More precisely, using econometric modeling in conjunction with the targeting information gathered in Chapter 5, I gauge the independent effect of group-targeting strategies on individual behavior. Examining individuals in cross section provides information about the effect that resources, characteristics, attitudes, and contacts with political leaders have on an individual's likelihood of participating. Adding contextual variables on targeted districts allows me to vary the strategic situation in order to gauge how the political environment influenced both elite recruitment and citizen participation.

Chapter 7, the concluding chapter, provides me with an opportunity not only to assess my theory in light of empirical findings but also to place the nature and use of elite mobilization of mass participation into a broader context. I discuss how my findings fit into the interest group and mass participation literatures and explain what my findings mean for specific reforms that have been proposed.

2

Patterns and Puzzles in Participation and Lobbying

The reigning theories of participation in American
politics, amazing as it may seem, do not have much
to say about politics. Instead, they trace activism to
the characteristics of individual American citizens,
to their educations, their incomes, and their
efficacy. They assume that attitudes determine behavior. When asked to account for changes in
citizen involvement over the last half century, these
explanations largely fail.
Steven Rosenstone and Mark Hansen, *Mobilization,*
Participation, and Democracy in America

When he was first elected to the Senate in 1958, the late Philip Hart of
Michigan received fewer than two thousand letters on issues each month. By
1975, near the end of his Senate career, he was receiving approximately ten
thousand letters per month.[1] In a typical month in 1995, another Michigan
Senator, Carl Levin, received more than twenty thousand issue letters, along
with five thousand telegrams, ten thousand phone calls, and one thousand
faxes.[2]

The increase in constituent communications to Congress over the last
three decades has not been confined to Michigan senators. As Figure 2.1
illustrates, there has been a dramatic increase in the amount of mail delivered to the House of Representatives over the past thirty years.[3]

---

[1] Author's calculations from the Philip Hart Papers, Bentley Historical Library, University of
Michigan, Ann Arbor.
[2] Author's correspondence with Senator Carl Levin's office. These figures do not include
other types of communications that a senator's office receives – such as requests for service
and information – but just communications that express constituents' views on issues.
[3] Calculating or tracking over time the volume of constituent communications that convey
citizen attitudes on issues to members of Congress is not an easy task. Students of elections
have virtually uniform access to precinct, town, county, congressional district, and state
results for the past hundred years. Although there may have been some fraud here or there

14

Mirroring this pattern, more than nine out of ten respondents (91 percent) to a survey I conducted of congressional offices reported record levels of incoming communications in 1993 and 1994. All told, almost 160 million pieces of mail (157,737,234 to be exact) were delivered to the House and Senate during the 103rd session of Congress according to the Congressional Research Service (John Pontius, personal correspondence, 1995). In addition, millions more Americans phoned, faxed, sent telegrams, and e-mailed Capitol Hill to convey their feelings on issues. My survey of congressional offices indicated that 43 percent of constituent communications were letters, 41 percent were phone calls, 12 percent were faxes, and 4 percent were

and some observers have questioned the methods by which eligible voters are counted, debates about the proportion of Americans voting range within 1 or 2 percent. No such statistics exist for constituent communications to Congress and estimates of what proportion of American citizens contact Congress to convey their feelings on issues vary greatly. Moreover, with elections, we not only know how many citizens voted, but what they voted on and whom they voted for. The House and Senate keep track of total incoming mail per month, but it is impossible to identify to whom it was sent, what it said, and whether it was issue mail.

Mail counts also do not include other ways in which constituents communicate with their representatives, and thus may understate the level of constituent communications on issues. Media reports and my own observations in Washington suggest that faxes, phone calls, telegrams, and even e-mails are increasingly the tools that citizens use to convey their feelings to Congress. Nevertheless, while these problems may understate participation, we must also remember that unlike voting, citizens can communicate with Congress as many times as they want. In sum, aggregate measures of constituent communications to Congress are crude ones that may tell us little about individual rates of participation.

There are also problems when we attempt to gauge rates of participation from the viewpoint of the individual. In the same way that public opinion surveys overstate turnout because of overreporting and the exclusion of low-probability voters from most sampling frames, public opinion surveys surely overstate the number of people who contact Congress. Also, although the "did you vote" question yields socially desirable responses, it is free of other types of measurement error (it is pretty clear what behavior the question is trying to gauge and when that behavior was done).

Since no data are available on the volume and character of incoming communications to individual congressional offices, I conducted a survey of congressional offices. Not requiring the responses of actual members, the survey was designed to be answered by staff members familiar with patterns of incoming communications to the office. In addition, to capture information from members who retired or who lost their bid for reelection in 1994, I conducted a phone survey of the offices of outgoing members of Congress immediately after the 1994 election. Unfortunately, the response to the initial round of the mail survey was not good (52 out 412).

A research assistant and I conducted a follow-up survey by phone of key committee members in the House and of the entire Senate during the fall of 1995. All in all, I received information from 112 separate House offices and 47 Senate offices. The data provided some basic information about increases and the nature of incoming communications. However, concerns about the reliability and comparability of the responses and the different ways that offices track their incoming communications make it impossible to use the data for any more in-depth analysis.

For example, some offices provided me with estimates while others with actual numbers. Some offices gave percentages, some gave raw numbers. Some counted postcards, while others did not. Some provided answers for the years asked, but many gave responses for incorrect years.

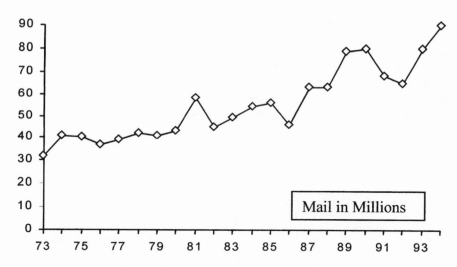

Figure 2.1. Mail to House of Representatives, 1973–1994. *Source:* Mann and Ornstein 1994, 164; Congressional Research Service (John Pontius, 1995).

telegrams. Also, according to my survey of congressional offices, more than three-quarters (77 percent) of the communications were from citizens conveying their feelings on issues.

Unfortunately, using these data, it is virtually impossible to distinguish whether this increase has been due to more citizens communicating to Congress or the same citizens communicating their feelings more often. Anecdotal evidence and conversations with longtime Hill staffers suggest that a significant part of the increase has been greater volume from the same citizens. Yet, these same staffers also believe that more citizens are writing.

The notion that more individuals are contacting Congress is confirmed by National Election Study data indicating that there has been an increase in the proportion of American's contacting their representatives in Washington to convey their feelings on issues.[4] The recent pattern is shown in Figure 2.2.

---

[4] The NES asks a two-stage question to gauge whether respondents contacted their member of Congress to convey their feelings on an issue. First, NES asks whether a respondent contacted his or her representative for any reason, and then specifically asks whether a respondent contacted the representative to convey their feelings on an issue. However, NES asks only whether a respondent contacted his or her representative in the House. The years included in Figure 2.2 are the only years in which NES asked the question of all respondents and not only of those residing in a district where an incumbent was running for reelection.

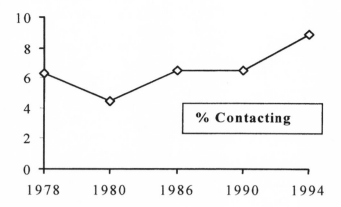

Figure 2.2 Percentage of citizens contacting Congress to express opinion on issues, 1978–1994. For coding, see Appendix A. *Source:* American National Election Studies.

Using the *Participation in America* data set as a baseline, Verba, Schlozman, and Brady compared rates of participation from 1967 to 1987. They found that the proportion of Americans reporting an issue-based contact with a national official doubled, from 11 percent of the population in 1967 to 22 percent of the population in 1987 (Verba et al. 1995a, 72).

Although Roper Center surveys (the longest available time series of communications to Congress) indicate a drop in "letter writing to Congress" over the past twenty years, the Roper surveys do not measure other ways in which citizens may contact their members of Congress. For example, Roper Center surveys conducted during the summer of 1994 found that only a little over one in ten Americans (12 percent) had written Congress in the last year.[5] However, Times-Mirror Center surveys taken during the identical time period showed that over one in four Americans (26 percent) reported having called, faxed, or written a letter to their congressional representative or senator in the past year.[6] Thus, when the survey question is expanded to include more modern modes of communication, rates of participation indicate a sharp rise.

Although it is virtually impossible to calculate exactly how many more individuals are communicating to Congress, data suggest a general increase in both the number of constituents communicating and the volume of constituent communications to Congress. Overlaid upon the trend of increasing

[5] Roper Center Surveys June, July, and August (N = 2,000).
[6] Times-Mirror Survey, June 23–26 (N = 1,021); Times-Mirror Survey, July 12–25 (N = 3,800).

communications to Congress over the past two decades are variations from year to year, district to district, and state to state. How can we account for both the general increase and these the accompanying fluctuations?

In one of the more robust empirical findings in political science, we know that higher socioeconomic status – specifically, higher levels of education – help citizens meet the nontrivial costs of participation and spur higher rates of political activity (Conway 1991; Milbrath and Goel 1977; Verba and Nie 1972; Verba, Schlozman, and Brady 1995a; Wolfinger and Rosenstone 1980). Yet increases in education levels alone cannot explain the rise in constituent communications to Congress that has apparently taken place over the past two decades. Moreover, they cannot explain variations from district to district and state to state.

Partisan attachments (Abramson and Aldrich 1982; Campbell et al. 1960) along with political interest (Neumann 1986; Verba and Nie 1972), efficacy (Abramson 1983; Bennet 1986), and information (Zaller 1992) have also been shown to be potent predictors of political activity. Nevertheless, at the same time there have been increases in rates of communications to Congress, all available evidence points to decreases or little change in partisan attachments, political interest, political efficacy, and levels of political information.[7]

In short, the most prominent schools of thought are unable to account fully for variation in rates of participation from time to time and place to place. It's not that this previous scholarship on the correlates of participation is incorrect. Rather, it is incomplete. Individual demographic and attitudinal characteristics are a part of the participation story but not the entire story.

The Paradox of Participation

Some citizens participate more than others and certain citizens participate only at certain times. A deeper question that many scholars have attempted to explain is why there is any mass participation at all? Virtually any type of mass political participation seems to defy rational explanation. To an individual, the costs of participation would appear to outweigh the impact that one's participation could have on the outcome, so why bother to participate? That is to say, since individuals can share in "collective" or "public" goods even if they fail to contribute to their provision, there is little incentive to engage in most types of mass participation. If my favored legislation passes, I still share the benefits regardless of whether I wrote my member of Con-

---

[7] Another part of the puzzle is that this increase occurred while rates of voting in congressional elections have declined.

gress. Only if the desired good is a "private" one, in which my enjoyment of the benefits hinges upon my participation, can we say that my involvement is rational.[8] If not, I have a strong incentive to be a free rider and a strong disincentive to bother to communicate with my member of Congress. This logic is represented by the following familiar formulation (Aldrich 1993; Downs 1957; Riker and Ordeshook 1968):

$$R = PB - C$$

where B stands for the benefits one will receive if one's desired outcome results, C represents the costs if one chooses to participate, and P stands for the probability that one's participation will be decisive in achieving the desired outcome. An individual participates if R is positive. Since P is usually very small and costs are not trivial, it is difficult to explain why people participate at all.

Previous findings about the correlates of participation do not provide a solution to the paradox of participation. In fact, they add to the puzzle. As Verba, Schlozman, and Brady argue:

Indeed, with respect to SES [socioeconomic status] and participation, at least one variant of the rational choice approach suggests no relationship at all or, if any, that people of high SES (who by virtue of their high levels of education command the intellectual sophistication to comprehend the free rider problem and by virtue of their high salaries would find the opportunity cost of participation prohibitive) to be the least likely to take part in politics. Instead those with high levels of SES, who are not otherwise known for particular irrationality in the conduct of their lives, are likely the most active. (1995b, 272)

Yet, just as a bumblebee flies despite the "fact" that aeronautical engineers tell us it cannot, people do participate in politics. To get around this inconvenient empirical finding, rational choice theorists have been forced to rely on other conceptions of benefits, such as the satisfaction gained from doing one's civic duty. However, this addition to the theory leads to a tautology in which people who participate in politics must receive civic satisfaction for doing so, while those who do not participate get no civic satisfaction from participating.

Nevertheless, these flaws do not destroy the utility of the rational choice calculus of participation. In fact, it has proved to be a useful tool in structuring arguments about participation and in identifying which factors influence individual participation. For instance, in the electoral context, more competitive races (with a greater chance of one's vote being decisive) have been demonstrated to increase voter turnout (Goldstein 1994; Rosenstone and Hansen 1993). This finding does not imply that individuals calculate their

---

[8] See Olson (1965) for the classic discussion of the collective action problem.

individual probabilities of influencing an election race. In fact, studies indicate people are no more likely to cast their ballots when they perceive the race to be a close one (Gant and Luttbeg 1991). Why then is turnout higher in close elections?

The answer appears to be that political leaders and campaign workers are encouraged by close races to work harder and to stimulate more voters. Thus closeness exerts an indirect, yet powerful, effect on an individual's chance of turning out to vote. Individual citizens may not care if an election is close; but parties, groups, and campaigns seek to invest resources where they will do the most good. Therefore, they are more likely to mobilize participation when a race is close. In this manner, although rational choice theories may not do a particularly good job in directly predicting individual participation choices, they may do a very good job in predicting campaign choices and in structuring our understanding of how the strategic environment can influence voter participation.

In Chapter 3, I argue that a similar logic helps us explain how organized interests make tactical decisions about lobbying between elections – about which legislators need to be targeted, which citizens need to be recruited, and what messages need to be conveyed. In a lobbying context, however, the costs, benefits, and probabilities represented in the rational calculus of a participatory decision are not identical for all individuals, all types of participation, or all types of political environments. The nature of probabilities, benefits, and costs will vary for different individuals who are deciding whether or not to contact Congress. These calculations are crucial as political leaders set out to make tactical decisions. Even if people don't use rational calculations in deciding whether or not to participate in politics, political leaders design their strategies and invest their resources as if they do.

A Mobilization Solution

In attempting to untangle the correlates of citizen participation, Verba, Schlozman, and Brady (1995a) distinguished between long-term causes (individual attitudes, attributes, and characteristics) and short-term causes, such as attitudes on issues. Not surprisingly, since they conducted their survey in the wake of the Supreme Court's *Webster* decision and the reentry of the abortion debate into the legislative battleground, the authors found that attitudes on abortion helped drive communications to Congress. The authors, however, generally discounted the influence of short-term factors in favor of a model that relies on more long-term explanations of participation.

In contrast to the more or less standing decision embodied by the Civic Voluntarism Model, issue engagements constitute a wild card with respect to their impact on participatory stratification. Their consequences for the representation of publics otherwise not well represented through participation are not fixed and stable. . . . As issues come and go, they mobilize to politics different issue publics. Because the issues that engender issue engagements are many and transitory, it is impossible to assess their net effect in reinforcing or counteracting the unambiguous impact of the structural factors in the Civic Voluntarism Model in creating participatory distortion. Nevertheless, the additional boost given to activity by an issue engagement is a small increment to a level of activity shaped more fundamentally by long-term factors. (Verba, Schlozman, and Brady 1995a, 522)

Earlier in their study, Verba, Schlozman, and Brady do demonstrate the effect that requests for political activity have on stimulating communications on policy issues. This finding is consistent with scores of previous studies on the impact of elite mobilization on electoral turnout (Cutright 1963; Gosnell 1927; Katz and Eldersveld 1961; Kramer 1970; Nagel 1987; Powell 1986; Wolfinger 1963). Still they argue, "The process by which people become the target of requests for activity is socially structured" (Verba et al. 1996, 149).

Although I agree that requests for participation are socially structured, I also argue that the process is politically structured. Short of understanding the "transitory" ways in which issues come on the agenda, short-term factors – political factors – can still help us understand political participation. Long-term factors certainly have a large influence on shaping participation and, as I argue, on tactical lobbying choices. The effect, however, of short-term factors is not simply a "wild card" having trivial, unsystematic effects. Political participation is a political act, with political goals, causes, and consequences. Issues alone do not mobilize citizens to political activity. Political leaders recruit citizens to political activity for political reasons.

Rosenstone and Hansen (1993) made a similar argument. They claimed that individual attributes cannot change quickly enough to explain changes in rates of political participation and that changes in elite patterns of mobilization can explain much of the variance in rates of participation. Although much attention has been paid to their claims about the role of mobilization in influencing voting and explaining the historical decline in turnout, Rosenstone and Hansen have also made a much broader argument about the effect of mobilization on political participation in general.

Specifically, they theorized that activities such as letter writing, petition signing, and demonstrating, dubbed "governmental participation," fluctuated according to the strategic decisions of politicians, interest groups, and parties. Using a thirty-year time series of Roper Survey data in addition to a cross section from the 1976 National Election Study, Rosenstone and Hansen demonstrated that the strategic choices of politicians, political parties, interest groups, and activists play a crucial role in determining who participates in politics and when they participate in politics. They argue that

"Personal characteristics – resources, perceived rewards, interests, and benefits from taking part in politics – define every person's predisposition toward political activity. The strategic choices of political leaders – their determination of who and when to mobilize – determine the shape of political participation in America" (Rosenstone and Hansen 1993, 36).[9]

If requests for political activity have such a powerful effect on individual behavior, we must understand what drives these decisions. We need to understand the less proximate causes of participation, the tactical decisions of political leaders. In other words, if requests by political leaders help drive participation, we must ask and answer the antecedent question: what drives these requests?

Interest Group Lobbying Tactics

Alongside the increase in constituent communications to Congress and consistent with the preceding discussion on the importance of recruitment and requests for participation has been a contemporaneous increase in the use of grass roots lobbying tactics. Specifically, interest groups and lobbying firms inside the beltway are increasingly making use of new and more sophisticated technologies to water the grass roots outside the beltway. To be sure, stimulating the grass roots is not a new technique. For example, around the turn of the century, the Anti-Saloon League had a mailing list of over 500,000 people and was the moving force behind the passage of prohibition (Odegard 1928). Writing in the 1920s, Pendleton Herring (1929) described the grass roots activities of corporations and interest groups during that time period. Going back even farther, Margaret Thomson (1985)

---

[9] Rosenstone and Hansen develop a convincing theoretical and empirical argument about the role of elite mobilization in mass participation. Unfortunately, in their models of "governmental participation," they face problems in operationalizing and measuring mobilization. In their examination of mobilization and voting, they are able to utilize specific questions to gauge whether a respondent was mobilized and are able to augment these data with contextual variables on competitive states and districts (where rational elites should concentrate their resources and mobilization efforts). However, in modeling the NES cross section and the Roper Center time series on nonelectoral participation and mobilization, they have neither direct measures of mobilization at the individual level nor direct measures of where mobilization efforts are likely to be targeted. The following variables were used as measures of mobilization in governmental politics: percentage of population that worked for political party; percentage of senators and representatives serving first two years of term; the natural log of number of bills introduced in year; presidential speeches in past week requesting letters to Congress; unemployment rate; presidential budget request as a percentage of last year's budget; number of days in session in past four weeks; and the natural log of the number of bills on the floor (Rosenstone and Hansen 1993, 266). These are creative measures designed to address a difficult problem and are likely measuring mobilization to some extent. However, all they measure with these variables can not be solely attributed to mobilization. For example, number of bills could be mobilization or it could just be that there are more opportunities or issues on which to write letters. Just as an election is an opportunity to mobilize, it is also an opportunity to vote.

found that corporations in the 1870s used grass roots lobbying tactics to curry favor with federal officials.

In their landmark study of lobbying and congressional decision making, Bauer, Pool, and Dexter (1964) described instances where particular industries and groups attempted to recruit employees and association members to write in support of, or opposition to, provisions of the Reciprocal Trade Act. Although generally skeptical about the power of interest groups to influence public policy, the authors described instances in which industry-orchestrated grass roots efforts apparently influenced legislative outcomes. In particular, they described how the American Cotton Manufacturers Institute (ACMI) organized millowners and workers to undertake a massive pro-protectionist letter-writing campaign directed at formally free-trade southern congressmen. The ACMI did not directly lobby southern congressmen, but attempted to influence them indirectly by recruiting influential constituents. The result was a shift in positions among traditionally free-trading southern congressman. Although recruiting influential constituents was apparently effective, Bauer, Pool, and Dexter opined, "the methods used by the ACMI to produce the 1955 shift were classic and unoriginal" (1964, 354).

More recently, Schlozman and Tierney argued that the increase in indirect lobbying techniques that occurred in the early 1980s was simply part of a broader increase in all sorts of lobbying activities. Respondents to Schlozman and Tierney's survey of Washington organizations reported using a wide variety of techniques and using them more frequently. In short, Schlozman and Tierney described a world in which the grass roots strategies and other lobbying techniques utilized by groups were simply "more of the same" (1983, 1986).

Still, of all the types of lobbying tactics examined in their study, the greatest increases occurred in outside tactics: "talking with people from the press and the media," "mounting grass roots campaigns," and "inspiring letter-writing" or "telegram campaigns" (Schlozman and Tierney 1983, 1986). Also, the fact that a tactic may be "unoriginal" or just "more of the same" does not mean it is ineffective or well understood by scholars. Furthermore, as Cigler and Loomis argue, "More of the same becomes at some point something categorically different" (1995, 393). Tierney himself admits in a later work, "In politics, as in oil spills or hazardous wastes, more of the same is not really the same" (1992, 219).

If the 1980s were more of the same when it came to grass roots lobbying, the early 1990s have been much more of the same. That is, it appears that grass roots lobbying is being used in different, more sophisticated, and potentially more powerful ways.[10] What can explain this increase?

---

[10] In Chapter 4, I discuss technological advances in much greater detail.

Kernell (1993) explained the rise in "going public" by presidents as a function of Washington politics moving from a system of institutional pluralism, in which bargains were struck by a few leaders of protocoalitions, to one of individual pluralism, where decisions were contested by an increasing number of free agents. The decrease in bargaining and the proliferation of outside strategies can also explain the rise in interest groups going public. The proliferation of subcommittees, the loss of power by committee chairs, and the weakening of the national parties demands that those who seek to influence public policy must now influence more policy makers. These same factors have also led to increasingly independent legislators who rely on their own actions, accomplishments, and skills for political survival. Furthermore, the long reach of the federal government and the rise of the modern welfare state have created constituencies outside the beltway that have an interest in the policies made inside the beltway. In addition, the growth of the mass media has made it easier for representatives and constituents to communicate with each other, and technological advances have made it feasible for groups to generate, virtually instantaneously, thousands and even hundreds of thousands of letters, faxes, phone calls, and telegrams when an issue or bill comes to a head.

Although it is difficult to measure precisely how much more frequently grass roots lobbying tactics are being used, and even more difficult to gauge their growth against some sort of baseline, there is at least some evidence, aside from anecdotal reports, to indicate that there has been a change in the magnitude and nature of such indirect tactics. For instance, media coverage of grass roots mobilization as a lobbying tactic has increased. Using on-line databases, I conducted a story count of the number of articles in the *National Journal*, the *New York Times*, and the *Washington Post* that contained the phrase "grass roots lobbying."[11] As Figure 2.3 illustrates, the number of articles about grass roots lobbying has increased dramatically during the past four years. After slowly rising throughout the 1980s, the number of articles mentioning grass roots lobbying tripled in the early 1990s.

Growth in the use of grass roots tactics by corporations and trade associations is apparently one major factor driving the increase. Whereas in the past American business and other interest groups were content to surrender the grass roots to environmentalists and other citizen groups, they have clearly learned about the power constituent pressure can wield on policy makers and have worked hard to influence policy through the use of sophisticated grass roots strategies (Dowd 1993; Mintz 1994; Vogel 1989). The

---

[11] The *National Journal* is the trade publication that most comprehensively covers lobbying and the behavior of organized interests in Washington, D.C. This finding should be treated with caution since different terms may have been used to describe political recruitment over the past twenty years.

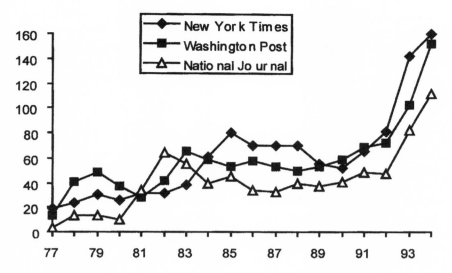

Figure 2.3. Grass roots lobbying mentions in the press, 1977–1994. *Source:* Nexis.

Public Affairs Council, a Washington-based group of corporate and trade association professionals, reports dramatic increases in the number of attendees at its annual conference on grass roots government relations techniques (Tony Kramer, personal interview, 1995).

Also, grass roots lobbying tactics are the subject about which the Public Affairs Council receives the most inquires. Moreover, most Fortune 500 companies now have full-time grass roots organizers and detailed plans of action that they can implement when needed. Efforts that were once ad hoc have now become permanent and official divisions of many corporations (Swift-Rosensweig 1995).

In addition, a whole new cadre of consultants who specialize in orchestrating mass participation has cropped up. Professional directories from *Campaigns and Elections* magazine show that the number of grass roots firms has grown every year and that more than 150 firms now specialize in stirring up mass participation.

These trends have encouraged a countermobilization (or a counter-countermobilization) by environmental and labor groups. Following the 1994 elections, the American Federation of State, County and Municipal Employees spearheaded a drive by organized labor – Project 95 – to place field organizers in thirty swing congressional districts. Similarly, the League of Conservation Voters placed field organizers in twenty swing congressional districts. During the August recess of 1995, the Democratic National Committee ran television advertisements about Medicare in thirteen targeted congressional districts that encouraged viewers to contact their member of Congress. At the same time the AFL-CIO conducted a million-dollar television and radio campaign aimed at twenty-six House districts (*Hotline,* August 23, 1995).[12]

Issue Advocacy and Independent Expenditure Campaigns

There is an important distinction between lobbying and advertising campaigns conducted more than a year before the election and the activities of groups during the electoral season. Think about the following campaigns conducted during the summer and fall of 1996.

Sierra Club, Citizens Action, and the League of Conservation Voters aired the following commercial during the summer of 1996 in the congressional districts of fifteen freshmen House Republicans. Over a visual of beautiful rivers and lakes changing to a visual of polluted lakes and rivers, the narrator made the following plea:

It's our land; our water. America's environment must be protected. But in just eighteen months, Congressman [name] has voted twelve out of twelve times to weaken environmental protections. Congressman [name] even voted to let oil corporations continue releasing cancer-causing pollutants into our air. He voted for the corporations who lobbied these bills and gave him thousands of dollars. Call Congressman (name) and tell him to protect America's environment. For our families, for our future. (*Hotline,* July 12, 1996)

There was no particular piece of legislation in front of Congress when these advertisements aired, and the call for action did not speak of any current legislative battle. Phone calls from environmentalists were not going to change the minds of these representatives, and there was nothing for them to change their minds about. The request for calls to Congress qualified the advertisements as issue advertising and provided a way for tax-exempt [501] (c) (4) organizations to engage in election advertising.

The respective parties' national committee also got in on the act. One of the most widely run was an advertisement by the Democratic National Committee. It featured ominous music and fuzzy black and white pictures of Newt Gingrich and Bob Dole vowing to let Medicare "wither on the vine." At the end of the commercial a phone number was quickly flashed and viewers were asked to get in touch with Congress. But the advertisement and the request for phone calls were not done to influence Dole or Gingrich. They were done so that these expenditures would qualify as legislative ad-

---

[12] John Sweeney ran and was elected to the presidency of the AFL-CIO largely on a platform of making organized labor a grass roots force.

vertising. The advertisements were targeted to swing states in the presidential contest and not swing districts for a legislative debate. They were vehicles for parties to communicate election messages before the campaign began and to evade campaign spending limits.

The GOP followed a similar strategy. The Republican National Committee aired an advertisement about Clinton "flip-flopping" on the number of years it would take to reach a balanced budget. The commercial ended with a quick request to get in touch with "your elected official." The RNC also aired the following commercial targeted at battleground states in the Midwest.

[*Woman and child are shown in doctor's office, with child on a nebulizer*]
Woman: I can't change jobs without losing my health insurance. Robbie has asthma.
    [*U.S. Capitol dissolves to shots of workers and patients being treated by doctor*]
Announcer: The Republican Congress wants to make sure workers who lose or change jobs keep their insurance – regardless of their medical condition. But liberal Democrats are blocking this commonsense approach [*picture of Ted Kennedy and Bill Clinton*]. And instead of giving people more choices, they still want government-run health care.
Woman: When are they going to learn that's not what we need.
Announcer: Write President Clinton and Senator Ted Kennedy today. Tell them to support the Republicans' commonsense health care reform.

It was unlikely that Ted Kennedy or Bill Clinton got much useful information from any communications stimulated by this advertisement. Once again, the goal was not to provide information to legislators or President Clinton, but to provide information to voters and frame particular issues. The goal was to put Clinton's picture next to Kennedy's in battleground states without exceeding federal spending limits.

My favorite example of a campaign advertisement dressed up as an issue-based grass roots lobbying campaign comes from the 1996 House race in the state of Montana. Citizens for Reform, a conservative group, aired the following commercial in the middle of the fall campaign (Carney 1997, 1643). The target of this commercial, Democratic candidate Bill Yellowtail, was not even an incumbent member of the House of Representatives. "He preaches family values, but he takes a swing at his wife. Yellowtail's explanation? He only slapped her. Call Bill Yellowtail and tell him you don't approve of his wrongful behavior."

Since this advertisement did not explicitly advocate the election of a particular candidate, it counted as an issue advocacy campaign, an activity in which tax-exempt groups are permitted to engage. Peter Flaherty, head of Citizens for Reform, explained, "As long as we don't use any express-advocacy words, anything we do is permissible" (Carney 1997). Similar reasoning allowed scores of other groups to air millions of dollars of advertisements – ostensibly asking for citizen action on a legislative issue – during the 1996 campaign season.

The stimulus for this project was a better understanding of how tactical outside lobbying decisions are made and how these decisions influence mass participation. Still, I do not examine all types of campaigns that request mass participation. Although some may consider the preceding advertisements aired in the midst of the 1996 campaign to be part of an issue advocacy campaigns, I do not. The use of independent expenditure and issue advocacy campaigns during an election is a topic that deserves further study. Nevertheless, even though the grass roots lobbying campaigns that I discuss rely on the electoral connection and may even have an electoral objective, the logic that governs their use is far different from the logic that governs the use of independent expenditure campaigns. These types of activities are clearly just another facet of a short-term electoral campaign and should be studied as such.

Chapter Summary

Many of the central insights of the mass participation and interest group literatures are correct, but they are incomplete. On the one hand, understanding why individuals participate in politics requires more than an understanding of individual attributes and attitudes. On the other hand, assessing the nature of interest group influence requires one to look beyond financial donations and the direct activities of Washington-based lobbyists. These factors alone cannot explain the explosion in citizen communications to Congress over the past decade. Likewise, traditional explanations of participation cannot account for this trend or the differences we see in who participates from year to year.

Requests for political activity play a crucial role in inspiring communications to legislators and are a commonly used lobbying tactic wielded by organized interests. Therefore to understand more fully both the nature of mass participation and interest group influence, we must have a better understanding of what drives these requests for political activity.

Nevertheless, based on the participation literature, we really know little about how tactical mobilization decisions are made. By the same token, traditional explanations of lobbying and interest group influence have concentrated on organizational factors and are unable to explain how grass roots lobbying is employed. In sum, to understand more fully both why people contact Congress and how lobbying influences the legislative process, we must understand how and why strategic and tactical lobbying choices are made. Up to this point, the lack of a specific theory about why and how elites make strategic and tactical lobbying decisions has hampered our understanding of both mass participation and interest group influence. In the next chapter, I take a first step toward remedying that deficiency. Although I will not tackle directly the question of interest group effectiveness, having a theoretical understanding of the logic behind interest group strategies and tactics is a necessary first step for evaluating their worth.

3

The Political Logic of Political Decisions

All animals are equal, but some animals are more
equal than others.

George Orwell, *Animal Farm*

Remember, there are only three people in Congress
who really care what your employees think: their
two senators and their representative.
   Mobilization manual from the chemical industry

Most scholarly accounts of interest groups and lobbying have focused on
how organizational factors and resources influence lobbying decisions and
choices of tactics. I start from the premise that political factors also have a
crucial influence. I assume that the architecture of the American political
system also governs interest group actions. Therefore, to dissect the specific
strategies and tactics lobbyists adopt in dealing with Congress, we must first
identify what factors actually influence congressional elections and congressional decisions.

   In the first part of this chapter, I take advantage of what scholars have
learned about elections and legislative decision making to understand how
and why grass roots strategies are used in lobbying campaigns. I argue that
grass roots lobbying is an effective tool for interest groups to provide – in the
way most likely to bias the process in their favor – the information required
by voters when they decide for whom to cast a ballot and for legislators when
they decide how to proceed on a particular piece of legislation. In the second
section, I argue that given the choice of stimulating constituent communications as a tactic, targeting decisions are a function of strategic objectives and
are determined by estimations of an individual's probability of influencing
the process. Given a particular strategic objective or piece of information
that needs to be conveyed, I explain the subsequent choices made by lobbyists about when to lobby, where to lobby, whom to lobby, and how to lobby.

Finally, in the chapter's concluding section, I derive a set of testable propositions from my representation of lobbying strategies and tactics.

Influencing Congressional Elections

Whether the objective is to influence current legislative battles or future elections, the lobbying tactic of stimulating constituent communications relies on the electoral connection and the manner in which issues affect electoral outcomes. Consequently, understanding the way incumbents' issue stands can affect congressional elections is an important first step in developing a theory of how grass roots lobbying decisions are made. Figure 3.1 illustrates the basic factors that have been shown to influence congressional elections.[1]

Congressional candidates whose party and president have high approval ratings are more likely to be successful. Democratic candidates in Democratic districts are more likely to be successful. High-quality challengers with sufficient resources are more likely to be successful. Incumbents who are free of personal scandals and have voted according to the wishes of their constituents are more likely to be successful.

Although national factors and the partisanship of the district certainly have a significant impact on congressional elections, given what we know about party identification and national events, they also are the factors that legislators and lobbyists can influence the least. One legislator can do little to make his or her constituents more Republican or the national economy stronger. Likewise, one interest group can do little to make constituents more Democratic or insure the successful completion of a war. Granting these basic determinants of congressional elections and the inability of interest groups to influence some of the most important determinants, how do lobbyists go about pursuing an election strategy?

Although much can be explained by these fundamental factors, campaigns are won and lost at the margins. Accordingly, interest groups can and do contribute money to candidates to conduct their campaigns. Furthermore, as discussed in the previous chapter, groups are increasingly conducting their own campaigns on behalf of friendly candidates. These campaigns can run into the millions of dollars and include all the trappings of the typical modern electoral campaign – television advertisements, mailings, professional field staff, and phone banks.

There is little subtlety to these supposedly independent electoral efforts or about contributing money directly to candidates. With these actions and

---

[1] The logic outlined in this figure is obviously grossly simplified and does not attempt to portray the relative magnitudes of the different factors nor the relationships between them. In devising it, I relied mainly on the work of Arnold (1990) and Jacobson (1992).

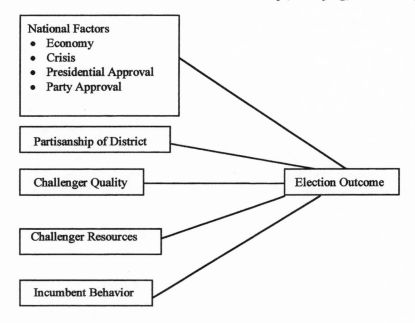

Figure 3.1. Major factors influencing congressional elections.

choice of tactics, interest groups are trying to influence voting behavior in the short term. Although the growth in independent expenditure campaigns suggests that this is a fertile area for future research, my goal is not to analyze how interest groups directly influence election outcomes in the short run. In this chapter and in this book, I concentrate on the indirect ways in which groups try to influence elections.[2]

Incumbent Behavior and Establishing Traceability

There is significant debate about the extent to which issues, particularly incumbent actions on roll call votes, influence congressional elections. Still, there are ways for organized interests to create the conditions necessary for issues and incumbent actions to have an impact. Arnold (1990) argued that for an issue to become salient enough to influence an election – for the behavior of the incumbent to be an important factor – three conditions must

---

[2] See Kingdon (1989, chap. 9) for a discussion of how interest groups try to tap into existing information flows in order to influence congressional decision making. Also see Rothenberg (1992), Smith (1984), and Wright (1996).

be met to establish what he dubs "traceability." First, there must be percep-
tible effects: gas is more expensive, taxes are higher, or sugar is cheaper.
Second, there must be an identifiable government action that can be linked
plausibly to the particular effect: import quotas on oil are approved, a new
tax bill is passed, or foreign sugar imports are allowed. Third, there must be
a visible contribution by a legislator to that government action: he or she
voted for import quotas, new taxes, or a sugar bill. Arnold (1990) argues
that when these conditions are in place, challengers can capitalize on the
actions of incumbents and particular issues can influence congressional
elections.

My model of how lobbyists influence election outcomes relies very much
on the logic outlined by Arnold (1990). But it differs in one crucial respect.
In Arnold's model, legislative entrepreneurs and the political environment
determine salience and traceability. For example, before an election campaign challengers or instigators determine which issues are salient and on
which issues an incumbent is vulnerable. I argue that more than legislative
entrepreneurs and legislative rules can establish or hide traceability. In my
model, in a legislative fight interest groups seek to define an issue and make
it salient for later use in an electoral fight. Interest groups, however, not only
react in the campaign season when an issue is salient and when traceability
has been established. They also may attempt to establish traceability long
before the formal campaign begins. Along with environmental factors and
the activities of legislative entrepreneurs, interest groups can influence
whether there is traceability on an issue. In other words, interest groups try
to provide the information required for there to be traceability on an issue
and for it to be used as ammunition in a future campaign.

If interest groups do not treat the traceability and salience of an issue as
exogenous, how do lobbyists go about highlighting policy effects and linking
policy outcomes to government actions and incumbent behavior? How do
they go about providing the information necessary to establish traceability?
Although groups can send signals with their monetary contributions and
professional lobbying contacts, stimulating constituent communications to
Congress is another effective way to provide information on electoral consequences. Lobbyists realize that how issues are framed in a legislative fight
influences how they can be framed in a future electoral fight. The legislative
battle over how a policy is defined can reveal much about who eventually
wins the electoral war. For instance, the outcome of the battle between the
parties and their interest group allies about whether a vote for the Republican budget in 1995 was a vote for a balanced budget and lower taxes or a
vote for slashing Medicare to provide tax cuts for the wealthy seems to have
had a significant impact on the 1996 elections. In that battle, mobilizing
hundreds of thousands of constituent communications and conducting a

television campaign in targeted states and districts seems to have been an effective tool for Democrats to frame the 1996 election during the fall of 1995.

Speaking of other legislative battles that preceded the 1994 election, David Dixon, a prominent Democratic media consultant and former political director of the Democratic Congressional Campaign Committee explained to me that "It is not enough to research a couple negatives on an incumbent, test which ones work the best and then make a great ad that airs a few weeks before the election. You need to be in the field, on the ground, stirring up opposition, enlisting allies, defining issues and creating defining moments long before the formal campaign period. Whoever wins the battle to frame an issue during the legislative battle will be able to use the issue most effectively in November."

Stimulating communications from the grass roots can be just the way to stir up opposition, enlist allies, and create defining moments before the campaign begins. Grass roots lobbying can be a most effective way for organized interests to frame issues in ways that make policy effects more salient, that make constituents aware of government actions, and that link legislators to those policy effects and government actions.

In addition, during a grass roots campaign, messages can be tested and groups can lay the logistical groundwork for an election campaign. Similar skills and resources are needed to mobilize people to contact Congress or to vote. Grass roots campaigns centered on a legislative issue can help groups to build an infrastructure, train operatives, and gather lists of supporters for future use in an upcoming election campaign.

Quality Challengers

Congressional elections are also determined by the quality of challengers. From their intensive case study of a single congressional district in upstate New York, Fowler and McClure (1989) argued that "The quiet calculations made by unseen candidates in February or March of a Congressional year or even earlier have as much to do with the electoral outcome in November as do the noisy fall campaigns." Simply put, those politicians who are well-funded and have prior political experience fare better than those who are poorly funded and have no previous political experience. To a great extent, who runs determines who wins. So, by recruiting strong candidates sympathetic to their cause and by influencing their "quiet calculations," interest groups can have an indirect, but powerful, influence on election outcomes.

Yet strong candidates who have the greatest chance of being successful also face the greatest risks (Jacobson and Kernell 1981). High-quality chal-

Table 3.1. *Strategies for Influencing Congressional Elections*

Objective	Strategy
Influence Congressional Election	Define issue and/or establish traceability for future electoral use
	Encourage or discourage potential challengers

lengers need to be convinced that a race is winnable. Krasno and Green (1988) demonstrated that local factors, specifically the behavior and personal vulnerability of incumbents, do influence strategic decisions about whether to run for Congress.[3] Encouraging constituents to contact Congress is one way for interest groups to demonstrate to challengers that an incumbent is vulnerable. Mobilizing constituents to contact an incumbent to express their displeasure about a particular action can provide significant information to challengers. Stimulated constituent communications to Congress are strong evidence that a winning message exists and that allies have the resources to deliver it. Stimulated communications may also show an incumbent that he or she is vulnerable and lead to the decision to retire. Similarly, stimulating constituents to convey their support for a particular incumbent's action can encourage an incumbent to run for reelection and thereby consequently serve to discourage potential challengers.

Summary

Previous scholars had difficulty documenting the direct effect of interest group activity on congressional elections. I have outlined a model in which grass roots lobbying can have an indirect, yet powerful, effect (see Table 3.1). Stimulating constituent communications is one way interest groups can prime the salience of issues and make it possible for an incumbent's record to be used in the next campaign. In addition, stimulating communications to Congress not only demonstrates to potential challengers that an incumbent is vulnerable to attack on an issue but demonstrates that organized groups are able to deliver important blocks of voters.

---

[3] I am agnostic on the debate in the literature about whether it is national or local factors that most affect strategic calculations about whether a race is winnable. My position is that local factors do have some influence on a challenger's decision.

Influencing Legislative Action

A logical place to begin to understand how lobbyists attempt to influence legislative decision making is to understand what, in fact, influences legislative decision making. As John Kingdon put it, "It is probably a general strategic principle that those who want something from decision-makers must adapt their strategies to the decision rules that are being used" (1989, 153).

Legislators have multiple motives when deciding how to act on an issue. These include the desire to win reelection, the desire to enact good public policies, and the desire to gain stature within the institution (Fenno 1973). Thus, when making decisions, constituents, their own policy beliefs, and the positions of colleagues and party leaders influence legislators. Without doing too much of a disservice to the volumes of research on congressional decision making, Figure 3.2 outlines what scholars have taught us about the forces that influence legislative decision making and the decision rules utilized by legislators. It shows what types of information legislators require when deciding how to behave on a particular issue. In devising this chart, I rely mainly on the work of Arnold (1990), Fenno (1978), Kingdon (1989), and Mayhew (1974).

Consistent with their desire to enact good public policy and gain stature within the institution, legislators' initial predispositions on a particular issue or piece of legislation are a function of their personal policy beliefs and the beliefs of congressional leaders and influential colleagues. Legislators also want to get reelected, however, and must therefore pay attention to the opinions of constituents. If a legislator's beliefs are in line with his or her constituency, then the decision on what action to take is an easy one. Also, as Figure 3.2 illustrates, when a legislator has no position or the constituency has no position (or has a divided position), then the decisions are also fairly straightforward.

Trouble arises when a legislator's initial predispositions are in conflict with his or her constituents.[4] But simply being in conflict is not enough to influence a legislator's behavior. Claiming that constituency influence matters and that legislators try to estimate their constituents' policy preferences does not imply that legislators conduct surveys and vote in the direction of the top-line results. Even if a member of Congress was capable of polling on

---

[4] Again, no claim is made that incumbent behavior is the most important factor in congressional elections. In fact, no claim is made about the exact influence of incumbent behavior on congressional elections. Instead, the more modest claim is that congressional elections are often won and lost at the margin and that personal actions are one of the few determinants legislators can control. Therefore, I assume that risk-averse legislators will attempt to maximize the benefit or minimize the loss from their own actions.

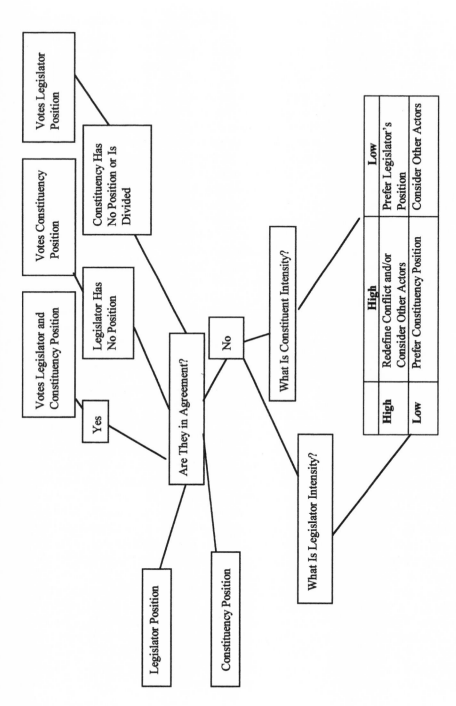

Figure 3.2. Legislative decision making.

every issue, the concern is not with the gross distribution of public opinion in his or her constituency. Legislators are unlikely to pay attention to even lopsided margins on an issue poll if they have no evidence that an action will cause politically important supporters to work against them.

For legislators to be convinced that a particular action could cause future electoral troubles, they need to be convinced not only about the general level of public opinion in their district but also that attitudes on a particular issue could potentially become salient in an electoral campaign and ultimately be translated into votes. Kingdon used the table in the lower right-hand corner of Figure 3.2 to illustrate how constituency influence and the electoral connection structure the choices of legislators when they disagree with constituents on an issue (1989, 39). If a legislator is not convinced that constituent opinion is intense (that opinions on an issue could be translated into votes), he or she is free to act his or her own way.

The level of pressure by party leaders and the depth of their own beliefs determine the intensity of the legislators' position, but how do legislators judge constituent intensity? How do legislators determine whether their action will have electoral consequences? Again, Arnold's (1990) work is helpful. Fundamental to his model is the claim that issues with potential salience can also influence legislative behavior. When a legislator decides how to act on a particular piece of legislation, he or she must first determine whether traceability exists and whether his or her actions on a particular piece of legislation could become a salient issue in a campaign for reelection. If so, a legislator must then attempt to judge how a particular action will help or hurt with particular groups of constituents and whether there are instigators who can capitalize on his or her behavior. "A talented legislator must ask himself only two simple questions: First, if I were on the other side, could I figure out a way to incite inattentive publics against me who voted on the wrong side? Second, are there, in fact, potential instigators who might mobilize inattentive publics against me?" (Arnold 1990, 70).

In sum, to determine constituent intensity, legislators need to know whether the effects of a policy are salient enough – or potentially salient enough – to influence large segments of the electorate. Moreover, legislators need to know whether there is an instigator who can capitalize on a salient issue.

If we accept this basic logic of legislative decision making and the informational needs of legislators outlined in Figure 3.2, how do organized interests go about trying to influence congressional decision making via an outside tactic such as stimulating constituent communications? Since there are multiple steps involved in legislative decision making, and multiple types of information required, organized interests have multiple options. Once again, the strategies are indirect but potentially decisive.

Providing Information about the Direction and Intensity of Constituency Opinion

The first section of this chapter discussed ways in which interest groups provided information to challengers and voters. Consider now strategies where interest groups provide information to legislators. One obvious option is to capitalize on the electoral connection and to provide information on the electoral consequences of particular courses of action. Grass roots communications are a particularly effective method of providing legislators with information on the attitudes and intensities of constituents. Vast amounts of constituent communications provide essential information to legislators, constantly trying to gauge how their actions will play out with constituents. Grass roots communications signal a legislator that a particular issue is on the radar screen and that constituents are paying attention to his or her actions. Grass roots communications can raise citizens' – and, consequently, legislators' – consciousness on an issue.

As Figure 3.2 illustrates, demonstrating that constituent opinion is on their side is a crucial objective for interest groups. In fact, in some cases, just showing the direction of constituency opinion can push a legislator in a group's direction. On many issues, however, other forces are at work and legislators need to be convinced about the intensity of constituent attitudes or, in other words, the potential that the issue will become salient in the minds of important blocks of voters.

Grass roots communications take some of the guesswork out of legislators' calculations of how their actions could be used against them or whether there are potential instigators. Stimulated constituent communications enable organized interests to prove they have both an argument and the organizational ability to spur constituents to act on a given issue. The information that groups hope to convey with grass roots communications is that if they can recruit citizens to write about an issue, they can recruit citizens to vote on an issue. In short, grass roots communications demonstrate to legislators that traceability has been established.

Framing Issues and Influencing Opinions

Changing how a vote is labeled or framed is also an effective way for lobbyists to influence legislators' calculations about the electoral consequences of their actions. In addition, winning the battle to define what a vote is about can influence legislative decisions by shaping the actual opinions of constituents and legislators. Most certainly, how an issue or roll call vote is debated is often a function of the environment or congressional rules. Still, as discussed in the section on electoral strategies, lobbyists do not necessarily view the terms of a legislative debate as exogenous. In fact, a large part of their job is making sure an issue is debated on terms most favorable to their side.

The highlighting of costs and benefits is an especially important goal of lobbyists. There are costs and benefits to every bill. Although legislative entrepreneurs and the political environment prime particular costs and benefits, communicating information to constituents and legislators is a particularly effective way to stress the consequences that best make an interest group's argument. In general, it stands to reason that an interest group would want to tailor its message in the most inviting and effective way. There is no law that says that the National Rifle Association had to lobby in opposition to the assault weapon ban with the same language or issue attributes that President Clinton used to support the law.[5] Instead of talking about Uzis and AK-47s, opponents talked about "pork" and midnight basketball.

Tens of millions of dollars are spent each year researching precisely what the optimal policy message is for a policy battle, and interest groups have many possible ways in which to go about framing an issue. Nevertheless, lobbyists are constrained in their ability to define what an issue is about. No matter how potentially effective their message may be, they also need a credible messenger. Grass roots communications can act as such a messenger. An official with an insurance association explained to me, "Newt and Haley Barbour [RNC Chair] can spin themselves into the ground on *Crossfire,* but you need real people to make the spin credible."

Grass roots lobbying can be an effective technique to redefine issues and influence legislative opinion. Consider the 1993 battle over reduced tax deductions for business meals. It demonstrated the capacity orchestrated mass participation has to redefine an issue in more politically acceptable ways. What policy or electoral reason would a legislator have to support a narrow provision if it mostly benefits restaurant owners and wealthy members of the business community? It is easy to picture a campaign advertisement in which lobbyists are shown dining in a fancy restaurant while a background voice ponders why Congressman Jones voted to protect a benefit for corporate fat cats.

In part, however, by using the grass roots, the National Restaurant Association (the other NRA) was able to replace this campaign image with another one – one in which a waitress from a small town in Maryland worries about losing her job and supporting her family if Congress approves this unfair tax increase. The script of the television advertisement went like this: "I'm a waitress and a good one. I'd better be because my three sons depend

---

[5] In the same way that using the term "partial birth abortion" advantages pro-lifers, using the term, "assault weapon ban" defines the issue in a way beneficial to proponents of the ban.

on me. But I might not have a job much longer. President Clinton's economic plan cuts business-meal deductibility. That would throw 165,000 people out of work. I need this job. . . . Call 1-800-999-8945 and you'll be connected to your U.S. Senator" (Dowd 1993).

Using this waitress at press conferences and in television advertisements, the National Restaurant Association organized food service workers (many of whom are women and minorities) to contact their members of Congress. Opposition to the reduction was no longer defending a "fat cat" benefit but instead was protecting the jobs of hard-working waiters, waitresses, busboys, and dishwashers (Brinkley 1993a). A tax increase was the message and working people were the messengers. Utilizing the grass roots, the NRA was able to demonstrate constituent concern and redefine the issue to its advantage.

The electoral consequences were reframed using stimulated grass roots communications. In addition, mobilizing waiters, waitresses, and dishwashers to communicate with Congress had a ripple effect and changed general constituent opinion on the issue. In this case, communications from restaurant workers even helped reframe the issue in the minds of some liberal Democrats who had previously been for the tax increase. The reframing of the issue also gave those legislators sympathetic to the restaurateurs' position ammunition to explain what potentially could have been a thorny vote in favor of special tax loopholes. Legislative entrepreneurs believed they had defined the issue and the votes in a way to prime populist passions and group benefits. Instead, in part by using grass roots mobilization, opponents were able to reframe the legislation as a jobs issue and influence legislative decision making on a number of different levels.

Summary

Working from an understanding of what influences legislators, I have identified three basic ways in which organized interests can use the stimulation of constituent communications as a lobbying strategy. Mobilizing constituent communications can provide information to legislators on the basic direction of constituency opinion; can demonstrate that constituent intensity is high, the issue is salient to important constituents, traceability has been established, and an instigator exists; and allows interest groups to frame or reframe issues, influencing general constituency opinion, legislators' estimations of how the issue could be used against them, and legislators' prior policy beliefs. Table 3.2 summarizes the ways in which grass roots lobbying strategies can influence congressional decisions.[6]

[6] The list of strategies is not meant to be a complete menu of lobbying strategies, but, instead,

Table 3.2. Strategies to Influence Congressional Decisions

Objective	Strategy
Influence Congressional Decision	Demonstrate the direction of constituency opinion
	Demonstrate the intensity of constituency opinion – reframe issue, establish traceability, or show that instigator exists
	Influence constituency opinion by reframing issue
	Influence legislator by redefining issue

Choosing When, Where, Whom, and How to Mobilize

When the tactic of stimulating constituent communications is chosen, judgments about the weight that an individual's communication to Congress will have on the ultimate outcome of a legislative fight determine tactical decisions about when, where, whom, and how to target. These judgments are based on the fact that, unlike votes in an election, communications to Congress are not interchangeable. Comparing voting, the most common and commonly studied form of participation, to contacting Congress is an excellent way to elucidate this point.

In an election each citizen has one equal vote, and the candidate with the most votes wins the election in that district or state.[7] The probability of one's vote influencing the election can be easily calculated. It is identical – and identically small – for all voters. This, however, is not the case with communications to Congress. The probability that an individual's communication will influence the process is not necessarily equal to his or her fellow citizens and is not necessarily small. Instead, it is a function of the individual communicating, the legislator being communicated to, and the content of the message.

to include ones in which a grass roots campaign is applicable. For example, Hall and Wayman (1990) found evidence that mobilizing participation in committee is a strategic objective of those who donate money to candidates. Grass roots tactics, however, are unlikely to get legislators to work harder in committee. Unlike PAC donations, which give a member resources, grass roots lobbying takes time and resources from members. Instead of working harder, a member who is the target of a grass roots campaign has to allocate precious staff time and resources to handling the incoming communications.

[7] Having grown up in politics in Massachusetts, I learned this much later in life.

For instance, with communications to Congress, not only can individuals contact Congress as many times as they wish, but the value of their participatory acts differs. Bill Gates's ballot for Congress counts the same as a graduate student's ballot for Congress. However, Bill Gates's letter to his senator more than likely has a higher weight than a graduate student's letter. In addition, although votes are anonymous, the identities of those who contact Congress are known. In fact the identity of the citizen communicating to Congress is a major piece of information that is being communicated.

Votes are also blunt instruments. They are constrained in their ability to convey precise information. No matter one's skills, everyone's ballot conveys the same type of information. Conversely, communications to Congress convey specific information about the attitudes of particular citizens on particular issues. Moreover, the value of the information conveyed in the contact is often a function of the skill and status of the individual crafting the communication. Finally, there are no fixed rules for tallying communications to Congress. Although the volume of communications a legislator receives may be important, legislators do not simply count – or weigh – the volume of incoming communications and vote the side with the largest number.

With different and not necessarily small weights for communications to Congress, it stands to reason that interest groups would want to recruit those with the highest weights. Given a particular strategy and a particular type of information that needs to be conveyed, groups striving to maximize their influence should recruit those with the greatest probability of helping them achieve their objective. But, with no fixed weights and no fixed rules for tallying, how do lobbyists go about contacting those with the greatest probability of helping them achieve their strategic objective? How are weights calculated and decisions made about when, where, whom, and how to stimulate constituent communications to Congress?[8] What factors influence the value or weight of a communication to Congress?

With a legislative objective, the essential insight necessary to answer these questions is that all constituents are not equal and that all legislators are not equal. The influence of a communication on the policy process is a function of the individual communicating, the legislator being communicated to, and the message needing to be communicated. Since individual citizens are

---

[8] Strategic choices also may be restricted by a group's ability to execute the required tactics. Reframing an issue to change public opinion may be the best strategy, but a group may not have a credible way to do that. Establishing traceability for swing votes on the Senate Finance Committee may be the best strategy, but a group may have no members in that state or no resources to conduct a grass roots lobbying campaign. In addition, answers to the "when, where, whom, and how" questions of mobilization also depend on each other. Who is mobilized within a district depends on the member targeted; how a mobilization campaign is conducted depends on whom groups need to mobilize.

simultaneously recipients and transmitters of strategically targeted elite pressure, information about the goals of lobbyists and the characteristics of citizens and legislators needs to be combined in order to calculate a weight.

More specifically, a citizen's probability of influencing the process is a function of four factors: the probability that an individual citizen's input will influence a legislator, the probability that a legislator's behavior will influence the ultimate policy output, the probability that a citizen will participate if asked, and the probability that a citizen will convey the proper message. The argument can be represented by the following equation:

$$W = (IL \times OL \times IC \times PP) \times D$$

where W is an individual's recruitment weight, IL is the influence of a legislator on the policy process, OL is the openness of a legislator to persuasion, IC is the influence of a citizen on that legislator, PP is the probability that a citizen will contact the legislator if asked, and D is the direction of the information the citizen will convey. Assuming that interest groups are rational actors wanting to maximize their influence on the policy process, we should expect groups to target those citizens with the highest positive weights. Examining in greater detail what factors influence these probabilities can generate empirically testable predictions about lobbyists' choices with respect to stimulating communications to Congress.

With an electoral objective, the probability of a citizen's communication helping a group in the long run by influencing an election outcome is a function of a set of slightly different factors: a legislator's ideology or position vis-à-vis the group, the electoral vulnerability of a legislator, the credibility of a citizen in conveying a message, the probability that a citizen will participate if asked, and the probability that a citizen will convey the proper message. It can be represented by the following equation.

$$W = (ID \times V \times C \times PP) \times D$$

where W is once again an individual's mobilization weight, ID is a legislator's ideology, V is the electoral vulnerability of a legislator, C is the credibility, PP is the probability that a citizen will contact the legislator if asked, and D is the direction of the information the citizen will convey. Once again, assuming that interest groups are rational actors wanting to maximize their influence on the policy process, we should expect groups to target those citizens with the highest positive weights.

Calculating the Influence of a Citizen

Consistent with Fenno's theory about concentric constituencies, lobbyists know that legislators are likely to give more weight to certain communications than to others (1978). As one Senate staff member explained frankly, "There are constituents and then there are constituents." A single letter from an important member of an important constituency is likely to carry more weight than a single letter from an unknown member of a less significant constituency and, perhaps, even more than many letters.

Depending on their place in a legislator's district view, a letter from a local leader (banker, Rotary Club president, CEO of a local manufacturing firm) is likely to carry the most weight. Not only are these types of people more likely to vote, but they are more likely to be in a position to contribute other resources and to influence other citizens. Although they represent only three individuals, few legislators would want to be in conflict with constituents who have the resources and skills to influence other voters.

Since the value of a contact depends on the strategic objective, there are, however, exceptions to this rule. For instance, lobbyists hoping to reframe issues are often better served by recruiting less high-profile constituents. In the previously discussed case of grass roots lobbying around tax deductibility of business lunches, the goal was to reframe the issue. Consequently, to be credible it was necessary for the National Restaurant Association to mobilize low-income food service workers.

Conventional wisdom has held that "sincere" spontaneous communications are most likely to influence a legislator. Yet, this view is not consistent with our understanding of congressional elections, congressional decisions, and the informational needs of legislators. A communication stimulated by an interest group may carry more weight than a spontaneous communication because it carries more information. A stimulated communication may matter more because a group's organizational ability and intensity are key pieces of information that are also being relayed.

Calculating the Effect of a Communication on a Legislator

With a legislative objective, the probability that an individual citizen's input will influence a legislator is also a function of the legislator being contacted. Characteristics of legislators affect the probability that they will be swayed by information contained in the communication. A core assumption in my argument is that the electoral connection matters in legislative decision making and that communications are an important indicator of intensity and organizational ability. But I am not claiming that electoral considerations and constituent communications determine congressional behavior exclusively. Party pressure, previous positions, personal beliefs, and peer influence are also key components in the decision-making process of legislators (Kingdon 1989).

Legislators with a long public record in favor of a certain piece of legislation or who are beholden to powerful committee chairs will be minimally influenced by communications in opposition to or support of an issue. They are probably not good targets for groups pursuing a short-term strategy of influencing legislative votes. Senator Ted Kennedy of Massachusetts, a long time supporter of national health care, would not have been a good target for groups mobilizing mass participation around health care reform. Likewise, Senator Phil Gramm of Texas, who said that the Clintons' health care reform plan would pass over his "cold, dead political body" would also not have been a good target. Both men had solid, well-developed positions and were out of play.

Considering the broader topic of legislative targets, there has been an enduring debate in the lobbying literature about whether interest groups should focus on their friends or enemies. Most studies of inside lobbying hypothesize that groups either try to convert legislators – get them to do something they ordinarily would not do – or try to mobilize supporters.[9] In my model, tactical targeting decisions depend on the strategies and objectives being pursued. With grass roots tactics being used in pursuit of a legislative objective, it is the middle that matters. Lobbyists should target undecided legislators.

However, even with the particular tactic of stimulating constituent communications, other factors are at play and the choice of targets really depends on an interest group's ultimate goal. There are instances in which interest groups encourage citizens to contact a legislator even when they know their efforts will have little or no immediate influence on the outcome of current legislative battles. As discussed previously, messages delivered in grass roots campaigns are often used to soften up the ground for future electoral use. Thus, while certain legislators may not be good targets if a group's goal is simply to win the current policy battle, they may be targeted so that the issue can be more effectively used against them in a future electoral campaign.

In this case, the probability of a communication being decisive is a function of the electoral situation of the legislator and his or her position on issues of interest to the group. To use their resources most efficiently, we should expect interest groups to target those legislators in swing districts where, at the margin, their action on a particular issue has the potential to be decisive. Similarly, in working to encourage high-quality challengers to take on a troublesome incumbent, legislators in marginal seats should once again be the most likely targets.

---

[9] For a particularly intense "discussion" of whether lobbyists concentrate on their friends or their enemies and what is the best way to study that question, see Austen-Smith and Wright (1994, 1996) and Baumgartner and Leech (1996a, 1996b).

In short, while other studies have tried to determine whether lobbyists contact friends or enemies, I argue that tactical targeting choices depend on the strategic objective and the tactic being used. In a grass roots campaign with a legislative objective, targets are likely to be undecideds. In a grass roots campaign with an electoral objective, targets are likely to be persistent opponents in vulnerable seats.

Calculating a Legislator's Probability of Influencing the Process

For groups pursuing a legislative or vote-influencing strategy, the probability of a communication being decisive is also a function of various characteristics of the legislator being lobbied. Winning a skirmish with grass roots communications involves convincing a particular legislator to act in a particular way. Winning a war with grass roots communications involves getting a particular piece of legislation passed, blocked, or shaped in a certain way.

From the vantage point of elite lobbyists, the probability of influencing the process should not be thought of as the probability of a communication influencing a single legislator to take a particular action, but instead, as the probability of the communication being decisive in shaping the final legislative outcome. Depending on the stage of the legislative process, certain legislators are more important and will be targeted by interest groups. In the same way that there are constituents and then there are constituents, there are legislators and then there are legislators. Elite mobilizers do not simply aim to influence legislators; they aim to influence influential legislators.

A legislator's strategic importance can be judged in many ways. In the early stages of a legislative battle, influential and persuadable legislators on key committees should be prime targets for lobbyists. These legislators can be in positions of committee leadership or can be undecided votes. Early in the process lobbyists know the crucial battle is whether a bill emerges out of committee and what shape it takes. Thus, they will concentrate on legislators who can influence the form of the bill (Romer and Rosenthal 1978).

Certain committees are not only the relevant committees for many types of important legislation but are also considered to be cue givers to the body as a whole. We would expect the constituents of members of these committees to be more likely to be contacted than the constituents of noncommittee members. Also, as a bill moves to the floors of the various bodies, lobbyists should focus their attention on undecided legislators and their constituents. In addition, consistent with Kingdon's findings, certain legislators are cue givers for their colleagues (1989). Former senator of Georgia Sam Nunn was an example of a senator who was considered a key cue giver to conservative southern Democrats on all issues and to all senators on defense issues.

Table 3.3. *Objectives, Strategies, and Legislative Targets*

Objective	Strategy	Legislative Targets
Influence Congressional Decision	Demonstrate the direction of constituency opinion	Undecideds, key committee members, leadership, cue givers
	Demonstrate the intensity of constituency opinion – establish traceability and show that instigator exists	Undecideds, key committee members, leadership, cue givers
	Influence constituency opinion by redefining issue	Undecideds, key committee members, leadership, cue givers
	Influence legislator by redefining issue	Undecideds, key committee members, leadership, cue givers
Influence Congressional Election	Define issue and/or establish traceability for future electoral use	Opponents in marginal seats
	Encourage potential challengers	Opponents in marginal seats
	Define issue and/or establish traceability for future electoral use	Supporters in marginal seats
	Discourage potential challengers	Supporters in marginal seats

Depending on the issue, lobbyists should therefore try to stimulate lobbying activity among constituents of key cue givers (Mathews and Stimson 1975).

In Table 3.3 I connect the different strategies to tactical decisions about where to target.

Calculating and Influencing the Probability That a Citizen Will Contact Congress

Although there is no registration requirement or legal cost for those who want to contact their legislators, there is also no official structure for participating. Citizens must know more and possess greater skills to communicate with Congress. Prospective contactors must know a debate about an issue is taking place, grasp some basic details about the debate, know how to communicate these basic details, and determine whom to contact.

All in all, there is less socialization, less media attention, and no official structure for participation between elections. Therefore, to encourage participation between elections, lobbyists must not only provide an impetus to participate, but they must often provide the means to participate. No matter how educated, connected, and efficacious one is, a push is often necessary to elicit any type of communication to Congress.

Yet, surprisingly, just how recruitment contacts lower participatory costs has never been examined in detail. Although it has been cursorily examined in the electoral participation context, the focus has not been on how recruitment actually lowers costs. Instead attention has been paid to how contacting influences individuals' estimations of the benefits they will receive, the probability that their votes will make a difference, and their perceptions of the cost of voting. Using the rational choice calculus to describe the participation decision, Wielhouwer and Lockerbie argued that "The party contact may raise an individual's estimation of either P or B (or both) increasing that person's belief in the efficacy of his or her involvement or of the benefits accruing from the candidate's victory. Or the contact may reduce an individual's estimation of the costs associated with participation" (1994, 213).

My claim is different. In essence, I am arguing that stimulating participation between elections not only changes perceptions and provides a nudge for those already in a state of readiness to act, but it also creates the means to act. It is conventional wisdom among "get-out-the-vote" (GOTV) professionals – and has been demonstrated empirically – that mobilization contacts in the electoral context can increase voting rates by modest levels of 2 to 3 percentage points (Goldstein 1994). In terms of stimulating constituent communications to Congress, we should have much higher expectations about the effect of a recruitment contact. Contacting Congress is not a spontaneous activity. Citizens contact their legislators when someone asks them to and shows them how.

Although elite recruitment is a powerful stimulus, it does not guarantee participation. Interest groups should also seek to target those citizens who are most likely to participate if asked. Thus, because they tend to have more influence, and are more likely to respond to a recruitment request, we should expect citizens with higher levels of education and stronger connections to political life to be targeted. In addition, consistent with the claims of social psychologists, all else being equal, costs will elicit a more intense reaction in opposition than a benefit should elicit in support (Tversky and Kahneman 1981). Constituents likely to sustain direct costs as an immediate consequence of a particular policy should be more likely to contact Congress if asked and should be targeted by lobbyists.

Moreover, interest groups may not view as purely exogenous the likelihood that a citizen will participate if asked. By crafting their exhortations in ways that accentuate direct costs, interest groups may increase a citizen's probability of participating. Finally, lobbyists are not only able to facilitate participation by lowering the costs of participation, but by raising the costs of not participating as well. Professional sanctions to those with whom they have a business relationship and social sanctions to those with whom they have a social relationship can be brandished. It stands to reason then that groups would want to target those individuals in social networks and businesses over whom they have some leverage (Rosenstone and Hansen 1993, 38; Verba et al. 1995a, 139).

Calculating the Probability That the Correct Message Will Be Conveyed

As I have argued, lobbyists want to ensure that their resources are not wasted on citizens who will not follow through if asked or who will not have a large influence on the process. In other words, lobbyists want to target those with the greatest probability of making a difference if asked. Even more importantly, however, interest groups want to be sure that the citizens they mobilize will convey the correct message. As one lobbyist told me, "The first rule is do no harm!" It would be unfortunate for interest groups if they consistently wasted resources targeting the wrong districts, citizens who were not likely to influence the process, or citizens who were unlikely to contact their representative if asked. It would be disastrous for groups if they activated an influential citizen in the district of an influential legislator who conveyed information that helped their opponents!

Although the discussion up to this point has concentrated on how interest groups calculate the absolute value of the probability that an individual will contact Congress and that his or her contact will make a difference, the sign of that value is even more crucial. Interest groups want to make sure that the right message is conveyed, and we should expect reliable allies to be the targets of mobilization efforts.

Summary and Predictions

Tactical decisions are driven by the desire to frame issues and lower the costs of participation for those citizens who have the greatest probability of helping a group convey the information most likely to allow them to achieve a strategic objective. Consider once again the calculus of a mobilization weight when the strategic objective is a short-term legislative one.

$$W = (IL \times OL \times IC \times PP) \times D$$

To maximize the value of W, the probability that a contact will achieve a given strategic objective, we should expect interest groups and lobbyists to make the following sorts of choices about when, where, and how to recruit. Lobbyists should target likely allies, citizens with greater resources and greater influence, citizens in the districts of undecided legislators or key committee members, and citizens represented by legislators considered cue givers.

Now consider again the calculus of a mobilization weight when the strategic objective is to influence an upcoming election.

$$W = (ID \times V \times C \times PP) \times D$$

In this case, W is maximized by a slightly different set of mobilization choices. Interest groups should target citizens in those districts or states where a legislator who is at ideological odds with their group's positions is at risk and those citizens who can most credibly convey the desired message.

No matter the objective, mobilizers should target citizens who are likely to face early-order, direct costs of legislation as well as citizens in social networks or businesses where they have financial or social leverage. Mobilizers should also frame issues in ways that accentuate early-order, direct costs. Finally, no matter the strategy, we should expect mobilization contacts to have a decisive influence on a decision whether or not to communicate with Congress.

Chapter Summary

This chapter has provided a theoretical framework for investigating why grass roots communications matter and how they are used as a lobbying tactic. The structure of congressional elections and legislative decisions, specifically the need for particular types of information, provides strategic opportunities for lobbyists to influence the policy process. In the same way that legislators have multiple motives and thus require multiple pieces of information, interest groups have multiple ways to provide that information. Although others have also argued that interest groups strive to communicate information with their lobbying efforts (Kingdon 1989; Rothenberg 1992; Smith 1984; Wright 1996), I have detailed the specific kinds of information that stimulated constituent communications can convey. Moreover, working from the premise that targeting decisions are driven by the probability that an individual's communication will influence the process, I examined the tactical choices of lobbyists and derived a set of testable predictions. Different from other studies, I also took into account how tactics flow from strategies and how different strategic objectives demand different tactical choices.

In the following chapters, I set out to test these hypotheses and the political logic of mobilization from which they are derived. I test the predictions and explore how mobilization choices are made in two different ways. First, through interviews and observations of selected cases, I investigate the decisions of mobilizers to see if their choices are consistent with my theoretical framework. Second, I use surveys of the mass public in conjunction with information on targeted areas to determine who contacts Congress, who is mobilized, and the effect of mobilization.

4

Explaining Lobbying Decisions

Well, politics.
    Union field director's response when asked what
    factors influenced the union's targeting decisions

The three most important aspects of grass roots
lobbying are targeting, targeting, and targeting.
                    Trade association field director

In the previous chapter I laid out a theoretical framework to explain grass
roots lobbying choices. Using information I gathered on grass roots lobbying campaigns, I now begin the task of investigating if the actual methods
and lobbying choices of interest groups are consistent with this theoretical
framework. The heart of this chapter consists of data gathered from forty-
one formal interviews with interest group representatives. As discussed in
the Introduction, the unit of analysis in this data set is neither the individual
whom I interviewed nor the group he or she represented. Instead, the unit of
analysis is the individual grass roots campaigns and lobbying choices that
were made.

Altogether, the forty-one interviews covered ninety-four separate grass
roots lobbying campaigns across fifteen issue domains. Because of the timing of my study, campaigns connected with health care compose almost one-
quarter (22 percent) of all lobbying campaigns in my sample and almost
one-third (31 percent) of the lobbying campaigns with a legislative objective. Since I had sufficient cases and extra information on health care lobbying and so as not to overwhelm all the other issue advocacy campaigns, I
concentrate on health care lobbying decisions alone in Chapter 5. In this
chapter, I focus on the fourteen remaining issues on which I gathered
information.

In the first section of this chapter I examine the strategic objectives of the
various lobbying campaigns contained in my sample. In the second section,

I examine the tactical choices of groups in lobbying campaigns with legislative objectives. In the third section, I describe tactical choices in lobbying campaigns with electoral objectives.

Strategic Objectives

Tactical choices rely on the strategic objectives of interest groups. Tactical choices depend on the information groups want to convey with their efforts. More specifically, with a legislative objective, lobbyists strive to convey information to members of Congress on the electoral consequences of their actions. With an electoral objective, lobbyists strive to convey information to constituents that make it more likely that a particular legislator's action will be a decisive factor in an upcoming election. In addition, with an electoral objective, lobbyists seek to convey information to potential challengers that a legislator is vulnerable and that groups have both a message that resonates and the ability to deliver it. Again, as discussed in previous chapters, I differentiate between independent expenditure campaigns or issue advocacy campaigns that are conducted during the campaign season and those conducted with more long-term objectives well before the start of the formal campaign.

Of the fourteen issue areas in my study that attracted grass roots lobbying campaigns, five had a legislative objective, four had an electoral objective, and five had mixed strategic objectives. Issues on which a pure electoral strategy was at work included Medicare and the 1996 budget, worker safety, term limits, and meat inspection. A pure legislative strategy was in place with NAFTA, tort reform, and lobbying reform as well as with lobbying related to telecommunications and tobacco issues. The battle over the Clinton budget and stimulus package in 1993, partial-birth abortion, the crime bill, campaign finance, and the balanced budget amendment were issues that drew a mixture of strategies with some groups pursuing electoral objectives and others pursuing legislative objectives.

Table 4.1 reports the distribution of strategic objectives by grass roots lobbying campaign. An implied electoral threat is clearly a crucial part of a grass roots campaign with a legislative objective. Nevertheless, corporations and trade associations in my sample were unlikely to engage in grass roots lobbying campaigns with direct electoral objectives. Electoral objectives were more likely to be pursued by ideological groups and unions.

The majority of the seventy-three mobilization campaigns analyzed in this chapter (60 percent) had a legislative objective. Less than four in ten (36 percent) had an electoral objective. An analysis including health care reform campaigns would have skewed the distribution even more toward grass roots campaigns with a legislative objective.

Table 4.1. *Strategic Objective by Number of Mobilization Campaigns*

Objective	Frequency
Legislative	44 (60%)
Electoral	26 (36%)
Organizational	3 (4%)
Total	73

Source: Author's interviews.

As Table 4.1 also shows, there was another possible strategic objective – organizational maintenance. The groups included in my sample probably underestimate the amount of grass roots lobbying that goes on in order to build and maintain an organization. Again, no claim is made that my sampling methods provide information on the distribution of lobbying strategies.

Examples of Strategic Objectives

The legislative battle over NAFTA exemplified a lobbying campaign with a pure short-term legislative strategy. Although the electoral threat was explicit in union tactics, the immediate goal was to pass or defeat the trade agreement. Unions sought to convince members of Congress that constituent opposition was intense – that the issue was important to large blocks of voters, that traceability had been established, and that an instigator existed. Interviews with those on the other side of the debate suggested that the objective of many in the business community was to use constituent communications as a counterweight to the union efforts. In essence, there was nothing fancy about the debate over NAFTA. Both sides were competing to see who could convey the most compelling information on the political consequences of a particular course of action. A woman involved in the business coalition to support NAFTA explained:[1]

If NAFTA was a secret ballot, it would not have been close and we would not have had to spend any time on lobbying. But it obviously wasn't and members who were inclined to be with us were taking a pounding at home from the unions and the environmentalists – and from Gephardt and Bonior here in Washington. They needed an excuse to be with us. They needed some sort of signal that they were not going to be hung out to dry on this. We even had members asking us to get constituents to contact them.

---

[1] Unless otherwise noted, all data and results presented in this chapter rely on my interviews.

With the 1993 budget, opponents of President Clinton's plan attempted to establish traceability on certain elements of the package. The objective was to uncouple parts of the bill to highlight the short-term direct costs of the plan – higher taxes – as opposed to the more long-term and indirect benefit of deficit reduction. In short, opponents of the Clinton package wanted to frame the vote in Congress as one for higher taxes, while proponents of the plan wanted to frame the vote as one for deficit reduction and lower interest rates.

Even though the messages they were using were similar, different groups had different strategic objectives. Some had an electoral strategy in mind, while others pursued a more short-term strategy to amend or defeat the Clinton budget. In some cases, individual groups may have pursued different strategic objectives for different legislators. In mobilizing constituent communications to Congress about the Clinton budget, one group in my sample targeted certain legislators it thought could be persuaded and targeted others because it was an excellent opportunity to prime an issue for future electoral use.

In addition, the grass roots campaigns conducted during the summer of 1993 around the Clinton budget and stimulus package were also used as a tool to recruit candidates for the 1994 general election. The director of one right-leaning ideological group told me, "One year out is a key time for challengers, and we wanted to convince the good ones that there were issues they could use and members who would be vulnerable."

Dual strategic objectives were also the case with pro-gun groups in the summer 1994 fight over the crime bill. These groups targeted some members in an effort to sway their votes and targeted others to prime the issue for use in the impending fall campaign. The crime bill debate also illustrated how groups can use grass roots communications to redefine issues. For example, the National Rifle Association may or may not have been outraged by midnight basketball and dance lessons. The NRA leadership, however, knew that it would rather debate the relative merits of liberal social programs than the relative merits of an AK-47. As one lobbyist involved in the lobbying campaign around the crime bill declared: "The first rule of politics is change the subject." Although the NRA used Second Amendment rhetoric in its communications to gun owners, the more general strategic objective was to reframe the crime bill. Accordingly, the message to the general public was about midnight basketball, dance lessons, and pork.

Congress eventually passed both the crime bill and the Clinton budget, but by razor-thin margins. Although the Clinton administration and the Democratic congressional leadership won the legislative battle, they lost the battle to define these particular issues. In the case of the budget bill, the legislation was defined by its tax increases. In the case of the crime bill, its spending components defined the legislation. Moreover, because of the extremely close margins of victory, every member who voted for the two bills was susceptible to the charge that he or she cast the deciding vote. In the months preceding the 1994 elections, then Clinton pollster Stan Greenberg often talked about running the campaign with a three-legged stool comprising deficit reduction, the crime bill, and health care reform. According to another Democratic campaign consultant, stimulating constituent communications was one way that Republican groups and their sympathizers "sawed the legs off Stan's damn stool."

The Clinton White House apparently learned the lessons from the hits it took on the budget and crime bill battles as well as its defeat in the health care battle. Using many of the same tactics – commercials, speeches, and field organizers in key districts – Clinton and his interest group allies went after elements of the Republican's Contract with America. According to at least one published account and one deposition, the strategic and tactical targeting decisions were made right in the White House and were often directed personally by President Clinton (Woodward 1996).

The strategic objective of Democrats and their interest group allies after the 1994 election was identical to the strategic objective of Republicans and their interest group allies after the 1992 election. Groups stimulating constituent communications around the 1995 budget battle and elements of Newt Gingrich's Contract with America did so to frame the issues and establish traceability for use in the 1996 elections. The battle was over whether the GOP budget would be framed as reducing the deficit and saving Medicare or as slashing Medicare to fund a tax cut for the wealthy. (Of course, the fact that the two sides were only $30 billion apart over a seven-year period – less than 1 percent of Medicare spending – influenced neither the tone nor the political consequences of the debate.)

The not-so-subtle Democratic strategy was designed to put the Republicans on the defensive. The goal was to put Democratic challengers in position to use Medicare as a campaign issue as they headed into an election year. Also, most of these grass roots campaigns were conducted in the fall of 1995 when potential candidates were making decisions about whether to make runs for Congress in 1996. In fact, officials of three unions with whom I spoke were explicitly using mobilized constituent communications to Congress as a recruiting device in a few selected districts and states.

One final example illustrates how groups not only have strategic objectives on issues that concern them, but often take advantage of strategic opportunities when offered. An environmental group in my sample instructed its field staff to mobilize constituent communications and create a stir about GOP efforts to relax meat inspection procedures. This issue was not really one that was in the group's normal domain, and the targeted legislators were unlikely to be swayed by the communications. Nevertheless, this environmental group viewed it as a strategic opportunity to score some political points and define an issue for future electoral use. The group's field director put it this way: "Most of our membership are vegetarians and probably felt like meat-eaters had it coming, but the whole e-coli issue provided us with a great opportunity to score some hits and soften up a few of our enemies." The opportunity was especially attractive because many of the most competitive districts in the 1996 congressional election were in the Pacific Northwest, where concern about e-coli was high after an outbreak in a chain of fast-food restaurants.

Summary and Expectations

Interest groups have different strategic objectives when they stimulate constituent communications to Congress. A group's choices about when, where, whom, and how to mobilize depend on these motives and goals as well as the type of information it needs to convey. Given the types of objectives discussed here, to maximize the probability that a contact will achieve a given strategic objective, we should expect interest groups and lobbyists to make the following sorts of choices.

The forty-four grass roots campaigns with a short-term legislative objective needed to provide information to members of Congress on the electoral consequences of a particular course of action. In these campaigns we should expect to find evidence that interest groups targeted citizens in the districts or states of key committee members, undecided legislators, and those considered cue givers. In the twenty-six grass roots campaigns with a long-term electoral objective, where lobbyists needed to provide information to citizens and potential challengers, we should expect to find evidence that mobilizers targeted citizens in marginal districts or states.

Within these targeted districts or states, mobilizers should have targeted citizens who were likely to face early-order, direct costs, citizens sympathetic to their cause, citizens with greater resources and greater influence, and constituents in social networks or businesses where they wielded financial or social leverage. Finally, no matter what the objective, the messages used to mobilize constituent communications should have been framed in ways to accentuate early-order, direct costs.

Targeting Choices and the Legislative Objective

Targeting is a two-stage process. Lobbyists must decide initially in which districts and states they will undertake their mobilization efforts and then whom to contact within those districts and states.

Table 4.2. *Timing of Mobilization Campaigns with a
Legislative Objective*

Targets	Mobilization Campaigns
Committee Only	19 (43%)
Floor Only	10 (23%)
Mixed	15 (34%)
Total	44

Source: Author's interviews.

When and Where to Target

My first step is to look at the decisions about when and where to employ
grass roots lobbying campaigns. As shown in Table 4.2, my interviews revealed that interest groups with a legislative objective – passing, blocking, or
amending a particular piece of legislation in the short term – were likely to
target swing members on key committees early in the process as well as cue
givers and undecideds when and if the bill came to the floor.

Previous work on lobbying has suggested that committee-based lobbying
is reserved for insiders and has only the subtle objective of getting members
to work harder (Hall and Wayman 1990; Wright 1996, 45). My data indicate that outside strategies such as stimulating constituent communications
are also pursued at the committee level. As Table 4.2 demonstrates, over
four in ten (43 percent) of the grass roots lobbying efforts in my sample were
conducted only at the committee stage. Furthermore, more than three out
of every four (77 percent) of the forty-four grass roots lobbying campaigns
with a legislative objective targeted at least some of their efforts at the
committee level.

Considering individual legislative targets, my model assumes that tactical
targeting decisions depend on the strategies and objectives being pursued.
When the objective is a short-term legislative one, my model predicts that
undecided legislators should be targeted. Consistent with this logic, there
was strong evidence in my interviews that lobbyists did, in fact, target undecideds when their strategic objective was to influence short-term legislative decisions and their tool was to stimulate constituent communications.
Specifically, as Table 4.3 illustrates, more than eight out of every ten grass
roots lobbying campaigns with a legislative objective (82 percent) focused
their efforts primarily on undecided legislators. To reiterate, the claim is not
that undecideds are always targeted but that targets depend on strategic

Table 4.3. *Member Targets with a Legislative Objective*

Targets	Mobilization Campaigns
Supporters	4 (9%)
Opponents	4 (9%)
Undecideds	36 (82%)
Total	44

Source: Author's interviews.

objectives and that orchestrated constituent communications are likely to be directed at undecideds.

When the energy tax was debated, opponents focused their efforts on the state of Oklahoma, which had three powerful officials in Congress who were potential swing voters: Senator David Boren, and Representatives Dave McCurdy and Bill Brewster. During the debate over the crime bill, groups with a legislative objective targeted undecided moderate Republicans from the Northeast and conservative Democrats from the South and West. On NAFTA, the targets included twenty-three House members who had not announced a position on the trade agreement. In addition, pro-NAFTA forces put field directors in four states they believed would be critical: Oklahoma, Kansas, Missouri, and Texas. By mid-November, as more and more legislators took positions and as passage in the Senate seemed safe, attention was focused on fewer than ten undecided House members. With the debate over the Hyde amendment on public funding for abortion, targets included twenty House members who did not have a consistent pro-life or pro-choice voting record.

There has also been a distinction in the lobbying literature between inside strategies and outside strategies. According to the lobbyists with whom I spoke, however, decisions about when and where to pursue an outside strategy were made very much in tandem with inside lobbyists. Groups worked with their own lobbyists as well as other allies in both the legislative and interest group communities. The communications director for a major insurance company explained: "We work hand in glove with our Hill lobbying staff. That is how we know what the key committees are and who the key committee members are."

Finally, even though the following declaration requires further empirical study, more than a few respondents made the point that a major benefit of the access they get with inside lobbying is to gain political intelligence for use with other lobbying tactics. One trade association official summed it up as follows:

If I'm out playing golf with some congressman or I buy a senator lunch, I know I'm not buying a vote. I'm not even buying access to convince him. What I am buying is intelligence. He might tell me that he is undecided on some bill that concerns me. He might tell me about how other members of Congress or fellow committee members are feeling about an issue. He tells me information that I can then take back and say, "Hey, we have an opportunity here," or "Hey, we better shore up our support here."

Whom to Target

According to my theory, grass roots campaigns with a legislative objective should target citizens who have both the greatest probability of influencing a member of Congress and who are most likely to act in the desired direction. As discussed already, however, lobbyists target specific members. Therefore, the first step must be to match potential citizen targets to their correct political geography. No matter what potential impact a citizen's communication will have on a particular legislator, lobbyists want to insure that it is directed at a legislator who is likely to be influenced and to influence the final process.

Advances in district-matching software allow interest groups to identify the congressional districts of constituents and have played an important role in the rise of grass roots as a lobbying tool. One company's name in particular, Legislative Demographic Services (LDS), came up in many of my interviews. The firm entered the grass roots lobbying business through its work with the Republican National Committee during redistricting after the 1990 census. LDS digitized 8,276 federal and state boundaries, defining all the various political geographies (congressional district, state senate district, and state house district) in the country by their latitudes and longitudes. They have also digitized sixty million nine-digit zip codes (zip plus four) and matched them to their correct latitudes and longitudes. For those addresses that only have a five-digit zip code available, they use another set of software that matches street addresses to their correct nine-digit zip codes. In this way, with a high degree of accuracy, the company is able to match members, employees, stockholders, vendors, or lists of potential sympathizers to their correct legislative districts.

Judging from the information I gathered, once individual targets were matched to the correct district, lobbyists pursuing a legislative objective were likely to concentrate on citizens who had the greatest probability of influencing a legislator – targets that they typically dubbed "key contacts" or the "grass tops." As Table 4.4 illustrates, pure broad-based campaigns were utilized in fewer than one in five cases when groups were pursuing a legislative objective. Although broader-based grass roots lobbying campaigns were used in conjunction with more focused efforts about a third of the time,

Table 4.4. *Constituent Mobilization Targets with a*
Legislative Objective

Mobilization Targets	Mobilization Campaigns
Broad Based	8 (18%)
Key Contacts	21 (48%)
Mixed	15 (34%)
Total	44

Source: Author's interviews.

almost half of the lobbying campaigns in my sample concentrated solely on higher-end constituents. As I discuss shortly, however, there are exceptions.

Consistent with these findings, the interviews also pointed to the tremendous amount of resources directed at identifying those who have a high probability of influencing a legislator. One company surveyed its employees and stockholders to determine the extent and nature of existing political connections. The company's lobbying chief explained her reasoning: "The congressman may be a brother-in-law or sister-in-law of an employee. He may be a neighbor, a fellow church deacon, or, say, a fellow club member, [or] have his kid on the little league team. We need to know that kind of stuff."

Often, such tactics are described as mobilizing the "grass tops." Jack Bonner, one of the most prominent consultants in the grass roots lobbying game specializes in recruiting such high-profile constituents. For getting a community leader to communicate his or her feelings to a legislator on the phone or in writing, Bonner will charge from $350 to $500. For setting up a personal meeting between a high-profile constituent and a member of Congress, Bonner can charge as much as $9,000 (Stone 1993).

A lobbying director for a trade association described to me a software program she used that searches for personal and professional connections to members of Congress. The software was originally developed by a company working for the Securities and Exchange Commission to track insider trading. The software looks at multiple sources – club memberships, university alumni lists, and fraternity and sorority lists – to determine who might have a relationship with a member of Congress.

More commonly, groups matched up lists of political contributors and supporters to their rosters of employees and stockholders. A manual by the chemical industry on how to set up a grass roots operation recommends:

A Washington Representative should have a master list of people in the congressional district or state where his company has operations, and know who has supported members, politically and otherwise, and who has some influence. Those who have supported members financially and/or helped sponsor fund-raising activities are in a better position to request support than those who haven't. Members of Congress react to key people in their districts and states, through leaders and financial backers, and it is up to the Washington representative/lobbyist to determine who can best approach a member.

Consistent with expectations, groups do expend significant resources determining who has a high probability of influencing a legislator. I also learned that they do not necessarily take this probability as fixed. In other words, they also work to increase the probability that a communication will be decisive. Quoting from this same chemical industry manual: "The Washington lobbyist must urge field personnel, from regional vice presidents to local representatives, to get to know their Congressmen and Senators and become well-acquainted with Members' district personnel." A manual from a pharmaceutical company recommended that local managers "raise their political visibility" by delivering in person their firm's PAC checks.

In addition, the goal of grass roots lobbying campaigns is not only to encourage influential constituents to contact influential legislators, but as one corporate official put it, "To get people to contact Congress in a way consistent with your company's beliefs." Organizations want to be sure that they are not mobilizing employees who could convey the wrong message. For example, in the battle over NAFTA, two telephone companies actively stimulated constituent communications to Congress. They did not, however, recruit any of their employees who were members of the communications workers union.

Leverage

Lobbyists not only want to mobilize those who will communicate the right message and who are influential, but they also want to make sure that the targeted citizens follow through on their requests. To this end, they often work with those over whom they enjoy social or financial leverage. As Table 4.5 demonstrates, members and stockholders as well as employees and vendors were most likely to be targeted by interest groups to contact Congress.

Many corporations have formalized their employees' public affairs responsibilities. For instance, one company I studied expected its plant mangers to contact their legislators four times a year and conduct at least one plant visit for their member of Congress. Political activities are a part of each manager's own performance review. Said one corporate public affairs official, "We have some legal problems if we put lobbying in an employee's job description, but we make it known what we expect. We give people mone-

Table 4.5. *Constituent Mobilization Targets with a*
Legislative Objective

Mobilization Targets	Mobilization Campaigns
Members/Stockholders	19 (43%)
Employees/Vendors	11 (25%)
Third Party	7 (16%)
Mixed	7 (16%)
Total	44

Source: Author's interviews.

tary rewards and recognition for their political work." A major insurance company "strongly suggested" to its midlevel executives that they take a three-day course on legislative lobbying and grass roots tactics. During the debate over NAFTA, automakers worked through their suppliers to stimulate letters and phone calls in support of the agreement. In particular, Ford Motor Company worked through its five thousand dealerships (Stone 1994).

Ideological groups and unions also target those over whom they have financial or social leverage. A union representative explained how his union uses "peer pressure" to get people involved in politics. "People see each other at work every day and we want to make people embarrassed if they have not done their duty." The representative of a group that concentrates its work in the churches explained that "seeing your fellow parishioners taking part and doing so publicly creates a real pressure to join in."[2]

Finding Allies

Although the preceding data and discussion reveal a concentration on key contacts and people over whom groups had leverage, the data also show a significant level of targeting of nonmembers or nonemployees. One consultant talked about a third-party campaign he had orchestrated. The client was a major defense contractor trying to get Congress to approve the building of a new aircraft carrier. To determine where it had leverage, the first thing the consultant did was to study the firm's accounting lists of suppliers. He then set up a conference call with 425 of the suppliers and informed them that they would be expected to have their employees write letters, make phone calls, and conduct plant tours for selected members of Con-

[2] See Chong (1991) for an excellent study of internal group pressures and participation in the civil rights movement.

gress. He then worked with the firm's Capitol Hill lobbyists to come up with a list of eighty senators and representatives they needed to convince. Out of the 425 suppliers, 300 had locations in the targeted districts and states. These companies were then sent precise marching orders and materials on how to initiate letter-writing and phone campaigns. Included with the marching orders and materials was a memo outlining how much the defense contractor had spent with the supplier and what would be spent in the future. The not-so-subtle message was that their future business relationship would hinge on their enthusiastic participation in the mobilization effort.

Also, there was evidence of broader-based mobilization efforts. One trade association representative explained simply, "If you don't have credible messengers, you need to develop allies who will take action." Her point made the argument that a citizen with a high probability of influencing the process is not always wealthy or well connected. Credibility is also important. For example, in a previous chapter, I discussed how the auto companies hired Jack Bonner to find credible allies. In that case Bonner recruited seniors and Boy Scout representatives to contact Congress in opposition to provisions in the Clean Air Act. Although there surely was a place for the CEO's of Ford, Chrysler, and General Motors, the objective of the grass roots strategy was to provide information that was best conveyed by average people. In such cases, communications can also have a ripple effect.

The battle over tort reform presents a similar case. Insurance companies could not get out in front of the effort to change liability laws. Therefore, instead of mobilizing just insurance salesmen, they targeted educators, little-league coaches, and small-business owners who could convey information to legislators on their frustration over the explosion of frivolous lawsuits and the cost of liability insurance.

Groups also use different messages to stimulate different target audiences to contact Congress. A tobacco company felt that it needed more – and more credible – citizens contacting Congress on the topic of whether the Food and Drug Administration should regulate cigarette manufacturing and sales. The company's government affairs staff came up with a three-part strategy. First, they mobilized smokers with the "stay out of my life" message. Second, they mobilized small stores worried about more taxes and regulations. Third, and most creatively, they targeted gay-rights groups with the message that the FDA's preoccupation with tobacco was distracting them from approving new drugs for AIDS. The effectiveness of these efforts can be debated. Still, this example is illustrative of how lobbyists do not always target the most connected or the most wealthy to contact Congress.

When pursuing more broad-based or third-party targets, groups obviously want to make sure that targeted citizens will follow through and contact Congress and that they will communicate the correct message. Many of the interest group representatives with whom I spoke argued that previous behavior is the best measure of how citizens will react to requests for participation. Consequently, much of their energy was directed at acquiring information about people's attitudes and past actions.

One of the most successful consulting firms in the grass roots business is the same company that pioneered direct marketing of credit cards. It specializes in integrating massive amounts of data from different political, consumer, and demographic sources in order to find the most fertile and friendly targets for mobilization. If time and resources permit, groups will conduct surveys off these lists to determine which messages work the best and what type of political or demographic profile is most likely to respond to a mobilization request. (Obviously, these "Cadillac" methods cost lots of money and are used mainly by corporations and trade associations and not by citizen groups.) As one trade association official explained: "First, we research who our target audience should be. Let's say it's college-educated women. We then gather lists of college-educated women. We test what messages work best with college-educated women. We buy advertisements on shows that ratings books tell us college-educated women are more likely to watch."

Technologies and Making Contacting Easy

New technologies are used by groups and consultants to make contacting Congress as easy as possible and to lower the costs of participation. In the 1996 fight over Medicare, a union representative explained to me how his organization sent field staff to construction sites with cellular phones. "Patch-thrus" are also an extremely popular new technology. With this method, citizens are called and read a script about a pending piece of legislation. If they are sufficiently impressed to want to contact their legislator, the caller immediately forwards their call to the office of their representative or senator. The calls and the response rates are constantly monitored, and the most effective messages are honed.

The United States Chamber of Commerce has built an elaborate computer system and phone bank with the capability of contacting a group's membership when an issue of concern to the chamber comes up in Congress. The software is able to sort members according to their geographical location and business type. When an issue arises that is of concern to the chamber, the system is programmed to telephone selected chamber members in key districts. A computer-generated voice informs the contact of the upcoming congressional vote and offers three choices: pressing "1" sends a letter in the contact's name to his or her representative; pressing "2" sends a voice mail to his or her representative; and pressing "3" immediately patches the contact through to his or her representative's office.

A main tactic for the Christian Coalition is to use churches as a way to construct target lists. First, staff members gather church membership lists and match names to the correct political geography. Second, they match these lists to voter registration files to determine party registration and past voting behavior. Third, they conduct surveys to gauge more accurately the ideologies of churchgoers and what issues most concern them. Then, when an issue arises and they want to mobilize communications, they have data on participation patterns, ideology, and issue concerns. Using these augmented lists helps them insure that a request will pay dividends and that participants will communicate a message consistent with the group's beliefs.

The Christian Coalition also makes use of broader-based tactics. During the battle over the Clinton budget, it aired television advertisements in the districts of undecided Democrats. The message asked if viewers were sick of high taxes and invited them to call an 800 number. Software at the location where the numbers came in immediately matched the telephone number to the correct congressional district. A packet of materials customized to the state and congressional district of the caller was sent out the next day. Even more importantly, the caller's name was then put on a list for future campaigns.

Tactical Choices and the Electoral Objective

National political tides and the partisanship of a district have a significant influence on congressional election outcomes. They are also largely immune from interest group influence. Nevertheless, two factors that can be influenced by interest groups – the quality of challengers, and the way an incumbent's record is viewed, also affect congressional elections. As I discussed in greater detail in the previous chapter, grass roots lobbying is an effective way for interest groups to provide information to both the electorate and to potential challengers. More specifically, it is a way for groups to convey information that may increase the probability that an incumbent's voting record will be salient and that a troublesome incumbent will face a strong challenger.

As many of my informants said, for a message to resonate in the *campaign* season, it needs to be framed in the *legislative* season. A field director for a business association involved in grass roots lobbying activities echoed these points and talked more about the process of creating defining moments: "Even if our letter-writing or phone campaign does not change a member's

Table 4.6. *Members Targets with an Electoral Objective*

Targets	Mobilization Campaigns
Supporters	2 (8%)
Opponents	17 (65%)
Undecideds	7 (27%)
Total	26

Source: Author's interviews.

vote, it can soften things up for the future. It helps divert a member from their script, unnerves them, makes them say something stupid that can be used later."

Where to Mobilize

Consistent with the expectations outlined in Chapter 3, when the strategic objective was electoral and the goal was to provide information to constituents and potential challengers, interest groups in my study targeted legislative opponents. As Table 4.6 demonstrates, about two out of every three grass roots lobbying campaigns with an electoral objective focused on legislators considered by interest groups to be opponents.

Just being an opponent, however, was not sufficient to draw the attention of grass roots lobbyists. Groups, in general, only targeted those members whom they viewed as being potentially vulnerable and who were likely to be affected by their efforts. Vulnerability was often gauged by a legislator's previous winning percentage and the partisanship of the district. In 1993 and 1994, Republican-leaning groups targeted Democrats who had supported Clinton's budget bill and who represented districts won by George Bush in 1988 or 1992. In 1995 and 1996, the American Association of Retired Persons, unions, and the Democratic National Committee carefully targeted their grass roots lobbying efforts around Medicare at Republican freshmen who won by less than 5 percentage points in 1994 and who had a large proportion of senior citizens in their districts.

Informal conversations with a number of pollsters on the Democratic side indicate that the multimillion-dollar effort by unions in 1995 and 1996 to regain control of Congress for the Democrats also made extensive use of survey research to determine where to target resources and on which issues to mobilize. Surveys were taken to determine which Republicans were most vulnerable, as well as which issues voters found the most important and

Table 4.7. *Constituent Mobilization Targets with an Electoral Objective*

Mobilization Targets	Number of Campaigns
Members/Stockholders	3 (12%)
Employees/Vendors	3 (12%)
Third Party	14 (54%)
Mixed	6 (23%)
Total	26

Source: Author's interviews.

were the most upset about. In short, the districts that were likely to draw the fire of the Democratic National Committee and its interest group allies were the districts where a member was judged vulnerable and the population showed concern about potential Medicare cuts, changes in worker safety rules, or environmental regulations.

Whom to Target

As expected, with an electoral objective, citizen targets were less likely to be members, employees, stockholders, or suppliers and were more likely to be potential allies from the constituency as a whole. Even large membership organizations like unions went outside their immediate family. One union official explained, "Frankly, there aren't as many union members anymore and lots of them might vote Republican. Seniors are good targets and Medicare is a good message, so we're going with that."

As Table 4.7 demonstrates, with an electoral objective, constituent targets were less likely to be members and stockholders or employees and vendors. Instead, with an electoral objective, in over half the grass roots campaigns I examined, interest groups targeted constituents outside of their immediate memberships or corporate families.

Furthermore, with a long-term electoral strategy, groups were more likely to pursue broad-based targets and not just go after the most influential constituents. In other words (and not surprisingly), with an electoral objective the value of the probability that one's communication will be decisive was similar to the one-person, one-vote rule of elections. As shown in Table 4.8, in more than two out of every three of the mobilization campaigns with an electoral objective, interest groups had broader-based constituent targets.

Table 4.8. *Constituent Mobilization Targets with an Electoral Objective*

Mobilization Targets	Number of Campaigns
Broad Based	18 (69%)
Key Contacts	3 (12%)
Mixed	5 (19%)
Total	26

Source: Author's interviews.

Examples

The following examples illustrate with actual cases both the types of messages that were used and the targeting decisions that were made by groups to stimulate communications to Congress and frame issues before the start of the formal campaign in 1996.

A commercial produced by the AFL-CIO was aired in the districts of twenty-seven Republican first-termers who represented districts won by Dukakis in 1988 or Clinton in 1992. The advertisement was aired during the summer of 1995 featuring Ron Hayes, an Ohio man whose son was killed in a work-related accident.

> [*Man is shown sitting next to his wife*]
> *Hayes:* Our son Patrick was a good kid. A real hard worker. Two years ago Patrick was crushed to death in the feed mill where he worked. The company thought they could get away with breaking the law. Patrick was just nineteen years old when he died. Now the Republicans in Congress are cutting health and safety protections I know can save lives. If they succeed, more people will die.
> [*Chyron graphic of House member's name and phone number appears on screen*]
> *Narrator:* And they've voted to cut Medicare. And college loans. To pay for huge tax breaks for the rich. Tell Republican Congressman [name] to stop cutting health and safety so other families don't lose their loved ones. Tell Congressman [name] to stop attacking America's families. (AFL-CIO release, August 21, 1995)

Later that fall, as part of the Medicare campaign, organized labor targeted twenty-two GOP members representing swing districts and representing a high proportion of senior citizens. Even though it is impossible to verify their claims, a union official reported that they made over 500,000 phone calls in those twenty-two districts. Consistent with this account, the *National Journal* reported on December 1, 1995 that elderly groups targeted twenty-six House Republicans who won with less than 55 percent of the vote and whose districts had over 12 percent senior citizens.

Chapter Summary

The premise of this chapter was a simple one: to understand how lobbyists make lobbying choices, one must look at the actual lobbying choices of interest groups. Using data gathered from seventy-three different grass roots lobbying campaigns as well as a good bit of soaking and poking, I tested the theory of targeting choices that was outlined in Chapter 3. Although difficulties in defining and sampling a population of groups pursuing grass roots lobbying tactics certainly do not make this the last word on tactical choices, there was strong and consistent evidence that there is little unsystematic or transitory about the targeting and recruitment choices of political elites.

As conversation after conversation and decision after decision indicated, interest groups strive to deploy their resources in the most efficient ways possible. Furthermore, the methods and technologies that I discussed in this chapter illustrate the premium placed on devising the correct messages, finding the correct messengers, and identifying those most likely to influence the legislative process in the desired direction.

These messages and targets were a function of different strategic objectives. There was strong evidence that the need to convey different types of information to different audiences yielded different legislative and constituent targets. With a short-term legislative objective, organized interests targeted undecided legislators and the constituents most likely to influence those legislators. While these were often wealthy or well-connected constituents, the data also showed that credibility – and creativity – occasionally demanded nontraditional messengers. When the goal was to provide information to voters and potential challengers, targets were likely to be legislative opponents who were judged vulnerable. Also, with an electoral objective, the constituent targets were likely to be more broad-based.

In sum, this chapter has provided an overview of how political elites decide when, where, whom, and how to target. In the following chapter, I examine the same questions, but do so by taking a more detailed look at one particular issue – the momentous 1993–1994 battle over the Clinton health care plan.

5

Lobbying Decisions and the Health Care Reform Battle

Step one, decide who will be the key votes on the key committees charged with health care issues. Step two, mobilize small business owners who are influential in their states and districts and are willing to deliver our message. Step three, take the people from step two and aim them at the people from step one.

> John Motley, National Federation of
> Independent Business[1]

If you don't want government gatekeepers telling you what doctor you can see, call Congressman Payne at (202) 225-4711 and tell him to vote "no" on the Clinton health care plan. That's (202) 225-4711.

> Citizens for a Sound Economy,
> radio advertisement

Five days after his inauguration as the forty-second president of the United States, Bill Clinton appointed his wife, Hillary Rodham Clinton, to head a task force responsible for drafting national health care reform legislation. Clinton was making good on a campaign promise to tackle an issue that had risen to national political prominence in the wake of Harris Wofford's upset victory in Pennsylvania's 1991 special election for the U.S. Senate. Clinton pledged that the task force would finish its work and that he would submit his plan to Congress within one hundred days. Due, however, to a more difficult than expected battle over his budget plan as well as various scandals and staff mistakes, Clinton's plan was not ready until late summer.

Still, even with the delay, when President Clinton finally presented his plan to the nation in an address to a joint session of Congress in late Septem-

---

[1] As quoted in Toner (1994).

ber of 1993, the response was extremely positive. A Gallup Survey on September 24, 1993, conducted in the days immediately following the speech, reported that almost six in ten Americans (59 percent) supported the plan and that only one in three opposed it (33 percent). Other public and private surveys conducted at the same time manifested similar levels of support for the "Clinton plan." Yankelovich's research had 57 percent of Americans supporting the plan with 31 percent in opposition. The ABC News/Washington Post poll had it at 67 percent to 20 percent. Public Opinion Strategies, the pollster for the Health Insurance Association of American (HIAA), did not include leaners and showed that Americans supported the plan by a margin of 35 percent to 21 percent.

In the wake of the president's speech, Republican members of Congress were talking favorably about reform. Even the United States Chamber of Commerce was saying good things about the Clinton plan. After the first lady won rave reviews for her performance during initial hearings on the legislation, support among both the mass public and key legislators even seemed to rise (Clymer 1993; Martin 1995; Skocpol 1996). In short, during the fall of 1993, the passage of at least some type of health care legislation seemed inevitable.

This atmosphere stands in sharp contrast to the state of affairs less than one year later. On September 23, 1994, House Speaker Tom Foley, House Majority Leader Dick Gephardt, and Senate Majority Leader George Mitchell emerged from a meeting at the White House. The trio declared to the assembled press corps that both houses of Congress were hopelessly deadlocked and that health care reform was dead in the 103rd Congress. What happened?

Because of the intensity of the lobbying push surrounding health care legislation, many claims have been made about the potency of interest group efforts in killing the Clinton plan and thwarting passage of any sort of reform in the 103rd Congress. Some observers have pointed to the battle over health care reform as a typical case of lobbyists controlling the legislative process and determining legislative outputs (Johnson and Broder 1996; Lewis 1994; Skocpol 1996). In particular, much attention has focused on grass roots lobbying and the hundreds of groups that mobilized millions of Americans to phone, fax, telegraph, mail, and e-mail their representatives in Washington.

Ira Magaziner, the architect of the Clinton plan, asserted to me in an interview that "the most effective tactic against our program was grass roots mobilization and phone banks in swing districts." Dick Gephardt, commenting on the effect of various health care lobbying strategies, opined: "It's not money. It's votes. The common view is that all of these interests came in and intimidated people by either giving them money or not giving them money. I think money had little to do with the outcome. It's the political work they did at home" (as quoted in Johnson and Broder 1996, 195).

The grass roots lobbying efforts of the HIAA and the National Federation of Independent Business (NFIB) have drawn the particularly close attention of numerous media observers. The "Harry and Louise" series of television commercials produced by the HIAA became legendary in media and consulting circles and were credited by many – most prominently Hillary Clinton – with turning the tide against the Clinton plan. Meanwhile, because of its successful campaign to strike any sort of employer mandate from health care reform legislation, scores of pundits crowned NFIB the new interest group power on the block (Duncan 1994; Headen 1994; Johnson and Broder 1996; Lewis 1994; Scarlett 1994; Toner 1994; Weisskopf 1994a, 1994b). In fact, in typical inside-the-beltway fashion, the NFIB sent journalists reprints of many of the articles that claimed they killed the Clinton plan. These journalists then wrote even more articles about NFIB influence – which were then sent to yet more reporters.

Lobbying efforts in general, and grass roots tactics in particular, alone cannot explain the demise of the Clinton plan. Some of the credit – or blame – must go to an overreaching plan devised in secret, a divided Democratic Party, a determined Republican opposition, and a problem-plagued presidency.

My goal in this chapter is neither to assess credit or blame nor to gauge the exact impact of interest group activities and tactics. Instead, the battle over health care reform during the first two years of the Clinton administration can teach us much about how lobbyists use grass roots lobbying and why many citizens participated in politics during the 103rd Congress. Whether or not it was "typical" or "the most extensive use of grass roots lobbying ever," there were certainly intense interest group activity and intense mobilization efforts surrounding health care reform. Again, conditions – the salience of the issue and the volume of lobbying – may have been unique, but the strategic and tactical choices made by interest groups were not. Health care reform provides a good case study in which to test the empirical implications of my theory of mobilization choices.

The Data

A subset of the interviews I conducted with interest group representatives constitutes the major source of data for this chapter. More specifically, I use information from twenty-one separate formal interviews with representatives of interest groups who conducted grass roots lobbying during the battle over health care. The interest group representatives with whom I spoke did not comprise a random sample of all groups mobilizing constituent com-

Table 5.1. *Interviews by Type of Group*

Type of Organization	Pro-Clinton Plan	Anti-Clinton Plan	Total
Trade Association	1	7	8
Corporations	0	3	3
Left Ideological	7	0	7
Right Ideological	0	3	3
Total	8	13	21

munications around health care – and certainly overstate the big players. The respondents, nonetheless, offer a good mix of groups by type of organization, ideology, and their position on the Clinton plan. Table 5.1 reports the kinds of groups contacted and their positions on the Clinton plan.

To obtain additional background information, I also spoke with Ira Magaziner, the architect of the Clinton plan. For the view from Capitol Hill, I spoke with two members of the Congressional leadership – one Republican and one Democrat – who were deeply involved in the debate. I also spoke with four veteran Washington journalists who covered the health care debate – David Broder of the *Washington Post,* Cokie Roberts of ABC News, Steve Roberts of *US News and World Report,* and Marty Plisner of CBS News. My observations as a political consultant during the eight months preceding the 1994 election also helped to inform my analysis and place mobilization choices into their correct political context. (See Appendix C for a chronology of the health care battle and a summary of the major plans and events.) All in all, the information I was able to gather provides a relatively broad and deep assessment of the lobbying choices made in the battle over health care.

Strategic Objectives and Tactical Expectations

The main strategic objective of grass roots lobbying on health care reform was to influence legislative decisions. Although the battle over health care reform also provided an opportunity for groups to engage in some organizational maintenance or to define an issue for future electoral use, the primary objective of nineteen out of the twenty-one groups in my sample was to pass, block, or amend the Clinton bill. This is not to suggest that these groups did not have other goals and did not use other strategies and tactics. In fact, and not surprisingly, many of the groups in my study used a wide variety of tactics to achieve a wide variety of objectives. Personal meetings were conducted. Testimony was given. Dollars were contributed.

Since spending on health care comprises one-seventh of America's gross domestic product, the stakes were enormous. Typical comments from my interviews included: "This was a matter of life and death for our members." "We couldn't afford to screw around, the very survival of our industry was at stake." "We needed to kill this animal now."[2] So, given the high stakes and the immediate goal of influencing a legislative decision, how did groups employ their grass roots lobbying efforts? What type of information did interest groups hope to convey by pursuing an outside lobbying strategy that, in large part, worked to stimulate constituent communications to Congress?

Because health care was a high profile issue and legislators were facing many competing pressures, interest groups could not hope to win the battle by simply providing legislators with information on the basic attitudes of their constituents. Legislators were already receiving massive amounts of information from the White House, party leaders, think tanks, and the press. The challenge for interest groups pursuing a grass roots strategy was to provide *politically useful information*. More specifically, the goal was to provide legislators with information on the potential electoral consequences of their actions. One corporate lobbyist noted, "They had lots of people telling them lots of things and giving them lots of information. We had to provide them with the information that they really cared about, how this affected their bottom line, how this affected whether they were going to get reelected or not."

Simply put, legislators needed to know whether they would be held accountable for passing or defeating the proposed health care reform. In Arnold's terminology (1990), health care legislation depended on legislators' calculations about whether there would be traceability for enacting or not enacting health care reform. Although the political and economic environment as well as the skill of legislative entrepreneurs clearly would influence the nature of traceability on health care, interests groups also worked to have a say. Grass roots lobbying and stimulating constituent communications provided one way for groups to have that say.

One of the architects of organized labor's campaign for the Clinton plan summed it up quite well: "We had to tell our people about the benefits and get them to tell their congressmen about those benefits before the other side could tell them about the costs." A business opponent of the Clinton plan remarked: "We had to explain to members of Congress – through their constituents – what the Clinton health plan was. We couldn't let the White House do all the explaining." Another opponent remarked: "First thing we

---

[2] As was the case in Chapter 4, unattributed quotations come from my interviews, which were done on a not-for-direct-attribution basis. In some cases, when a respondent gave me specific permission, the source of the quotation is noted.

needed to do was change the subject. If the debate had been about providing health insurance to middle-class Americans we would have lost. Instead, we made it about cutting jobs and reducing choice."

These comments were typical of the ones offered in many of my interviews. Broadly speaking, the goal of supporters of the Clinton plan was to focus attention on the general benefit of guaranteed coverage for all Americans and to demonstrate the electoral consequences to legislators if no health reform was passed and if certain elements were not included. The goal of Clinton plan opponents was to focus attention on the many particular costs that achieving guaranteed coverage would require and to demonstrate the electoral consequences to legislators if certain elements of health care reform were enacted into law.

The agenda was essentially set by the Clinton plan. Lobbying attention on health care reform quickly focused on four basic areas: employer mandates, price controls, mandatory alliances, and physician choice. The challenge for groups concerned with each of these individual issues was to demonstrate that there was a constituency for their area of concern. In other words, the goal was to show traceability for a particular element of the health care debate.

Some scholars have assumed that with a legislative objective as such, changing national public opinion or getting people from all over the country to contact Congress was the goal of outside strategies in the health care battle. Therefore, when they find relatively little national recall for advertising campaigns like "Harry and Louise" or a weak relationship between viewership and negative opinions of the Clinton plan, they question the effectiveness of such outside strategies (Jamieson 1994; West, Heith, and Goodwin 1995). If changing national public opinion and getting people from all over the country to contact Congress were not the objectives of these lobbying campaigns, however, then the fact that such campaigns failed to do so misses the point about such interest group behavior. "We were trying to move congressional votes, not Gallup numbers," was how one lobbyists put it to me. Another explained, "We didn't need to convince all Americans or all congressmen, we just had to convince the ones that mattered."

At bottom, convincing the ones that matter is essentially what my theory of grass roots lobbying decisions boils down to. The theory predicts that elite recruitment choices should be driven by the desire to frame issues and lower the costs of participation for those citizens most likely to influence the ultimate legislative outcome. These citizens are the ones who have the greatest probability of helping a group convey the information most likely to allow them to achieve a strategic objective. More specifically, this theory predicts that groups striving to maximize their influence on legislative decisions

Table 5.2. *Where and When Groups Mobilized*
Communications

Targets	Number of Groups
Committee Only	14 (66%)
Floor Only	0 (0%)
Mixed	7 (33%)
Total	21

Source: Author's interviews.

should target influential citizens in the districts of those members who are open to persuasion and who are most likely to influence the legislative process.

Examining the case of health care reform, we should find evidence that interest groups stimulating constituent communications to Congress had targeted citizens in the districts or states of key committee members, undecided legislators, and those considered to be cue givers. Within these targeted districts or states, interest groups should have targeted citizens sympathetic to their cause, citizens with greater resources and greater influence, constituents in social networks or businesses where they wield financial or social leverage, and citizens who were the most likely to face early-order, direct costs. Moreover, the messages used to mobilize constituent communications should have been framed in ways to accentuate such early-order direct costs.

An Overview of Tactical Mobilization Choices

As Table 5.2 illustrates, all twenty-one of the groups in my sample reported that they mobilized constituents in the districts of members of committees that were charged with tackling the Clinton bill. In addition, seven of the groups also mobilized on the floor around the leadership bills that emerged in the summer of 1994.

Five committees had jurisdiction over health care legislation: Senate Finance, Senate Labor and Human Resources, House Ways and Means, House Energy and Commerce, and House Education and Labor. My theory predicts the grass roots lobbying should have been pursued in those committees that were both open to persuasion and had a high probability of influencing the ultimate policy outcome. So, which committees were both important and open to persuasion? Answering this question requires an independent measure of importance or persuadability.

In studying elections, surveys and ratings such as the *Cook Report* and *Congressional Quarterly* provide a measure of preelection competitiveness, while, after the fact, election results show how close the race actually was. Unfortunately, unlike election results, independent information on the importance and persuadability of a committee and its members does not simply come off a library shelf. There are no surveys of the various considerations bouncing around a legislator's mind, and a dichotomous yes or no vote on the floor or in committee tells us little about how competitive an individual legislator's decision actually was.

Therefore, in an effort to provide some independent yardsticks, I supply four measures (admittedly imperfect) of which committees were competitive and which committees were likely to convey the most useful information to the full House and Senate. In spite of the fact that the committees all had Democratic majorities, the proportions differed. Since Republican opposition to the Clinton plan was virtually unanimous, one should expect committees with less pronounced Democratic majorities to draw the attention of interest groups. Moreover, although vote scores tell us little about attitudes on specific issues and should be treated with caution, we should expect committees with more moderate compositions to draw more attention. Although not a guarantee of eventual support, cosponsorship of a bill certainly indicates an initial level of support for a piece of legislation. Therefore, committees with large numbers of cosponsors of the Clinton plan should have drawn relatively less attention. Finally, we should also expect committees that could not afford to lose the votes of very many Democratic members to have been the focus of attention. Table 5.3 summarizes information on the percentage of Democratic members, mean Americans for Democratic Action (ADA) scores for those members, the percentage of committee members cosponsoring the Clinton plan, and the percentage of Democrats needed to report out legislation.

Of the House committees, the Education and Labor Committee had the largest proportion of Democrats, the greatest number of cosponsors of the Clinton bill, and, according to ADA scores, the most liberal voting records.[3] Moreover, even with no Republican help, Chairman William Ford could afford to lose more than one in five of his Democratic members and still report legislation out of his committee. Conversely, the Ways and Means Committee as well as the Energy and Commerce Committee had memberships that were less Democratic, more moderate, and their chairmen (Dan Rostenkowski and John Dingell) could afford to lose fewer Democratic

---

[3] ADA scores are one of the most commonly used ideological ratings. Other frequently used ratings are those by the American Conservative Union and the *National Journal*. All the measures correlated virtually perfectly.

Table 5.3. *Measures of Committee Competitiveness*

Committee	Democratic Members	Mean ADA Score for Democratic Members	Committee Democrats Cosponsoring Clinton Plan	Democrats Needed
House Energy and Commerce	27/44 (61%)	77	10/27 (37%)	23/27 (85%)
House Ways and Means	24/38 (63%)	80	9/24 (38%)	20/24 (83%)
House Education and Labor	28/43 (65%)	85	15/28 (54%)	22/28 (79%)
Senate Finance	11/20 (55%)	76	3/20 (15%)	11/11 (100%)
Senate Labor and Human Resources	10/17 (59%)	87	11/18 (53%)	9/10 (90%)

Source: Author's calculations from *1994 Almanac of American Politics* (Barone and Ujifusa 1995).

Table 5.4. *Committee Targets*

Committee	Groups Mobilizing in Committee
House Energy and Commerce	20
House Education and Labor	4
House Ways and Means	15
Senate Labor and Human Resources	5
Senate Finance	16

Source: Author's interviews.

votes. In other words, opposition interest groups needed to pick off fewer Democrats to win in the latter two committees.

In the Senate, comparing the Finance Committee with the Labor and Human Resources Committee yields a similar picture. Finance Committee Chairman Daniel Patrick Moynihan could not afford a single Democratic defection if he was to report out legislation. Furthermore, the Labor and Human Resources Committee had more liberal Democrats and cosponsors of the Clinton plan than did the Finance Committee. In fact, a majority of Labor and Human Resources Committee members were cosponsors of the Clinton plan.

In total, these independent measures, taken together with my theory of mobilization choice, point to the Energy and Commerce Committee and the Ways and Means Committee in the House and the Finance Committee in the Senate, as the most likely targets.

The information gathered in my interviews is consistent with these expectations. As Table 5.4 illustrates, of the groups with whom I spoke, attention paid to the committees fell into two distinct categories. The House Energy and Commerce Committee, the House Ways and Means Committee, and the Senate Finance Committee received three to four times as much attention as the Senate Labor and Human Resources Committee and the House Education and Labor Committee.

My interviews also permit us to look beyond these quantitative measures. Both opponents and supporters of the Clinton plan gave me a similar explanation for the pattern of committee targeting during the legislative battle over health care reform. Liberal Democratic majorities on Ted Kennedy's Senate Labor and Human Resources Committee and William Ford's Education and Labor Committee insured that legislation mirroring the Clinton plan would be reported out of these committees. Consequently, supporters

and opponents alike paid scant attention to the proceedings in those committees. Four of the six different groups that lobbied in the Education and
Labor and Labor and Human Resources Committees were to the left of
center. Their goals were to add more benefits or get a single-payer plan
passed in the two most liberal committees.

When I asked an insurance lobbyist why his company did not target the
Senate Labor and Human Resources Committee or the House Education
and Labor Committee, he quipped, "We weren't going to pay any attention
to those people's republic committees. There were too many coconspirators
(i.e., cosponsors) in those committees." Speaking just about the House,
Johnson and Broder put it in a little less colorful language:

There were only two places to pass a bill that could pass the House. Ways and Means
was one; Energy and Commerce was the other. The third committee with jurisdiction – Education and Labor – was a liberal bastion; over the years, the big unions
that were major bankrollers of Democratic Congressional candidates, including the
National Education Association and the American Federation of Teachers, had
packed that committee with people of unquestioned loyalty. "Ed and Labor" was
certain to report both the administration bill and the single payer plan favored by
many of the unions. But Ed and Labor was well to the left of the House. It had no
jurisdiction over financing provisions and only a marginal claim on Medicare and
Medicaid, the major existing health care programs. It was not likely to provide
legislation the leadership could take to the House floor. (1996, 306)

From these accounts, targeting decisions made by groups were consistent
with my expectation that lobbyists were likely to target those committees
that were likely to provide the best information to their respective bodies and
most likely to influence the ultimate legislative outcome. My interviews
provided evidence that this really was the case. Interest groups targeted
committees where the outcome was in doubt and where their efforts could
make a difference.

Although the variation in committee targets is certainly noteworthy, the
general targeting of committees may not seem to be a very surprising finding. After all, as discussed in Appendix C, most of the action regarding the
Clinton plan occurred in committee, and health care legislation was never
even brought to the floor of either house for a vote. But when we remember
some additional particulars of the rules and procedures in the respective
bodies, the fact that there was any attention paid at all to committees provides evidence for an information model of lobbying and for my theory of
mobilization choices.

Specifically, Senate rules allow only one committee to have primary jurisdiction over a particular piece of legislation, and neither Kennedy's Labor
and Human Resources Committee nor Moynihan's Finance Committee
was willing to cede responsibility. According to a number of accounts,
George Mitchell planned to use his power under Senate rules as majority

leader to bring health care legislation directly to the floor. On the House side, the leadership could work through the Rules Committee to reshape any bill that was voted out of any committee (*Congressional Quarterly Almanac* 1994, 320). The Education and Labor Committee was virtually guaranteed to report out a bill that could be shaped by Majority Leader Gephardt and Speaker Foley in the House. Why then bother to mobilize constituent communications during the committee stage?

The explanation is that committees provide information and are not simply procedural hurdles that need to be surmounted. In addition to passing and shaping legislation, the mandate of a committee is to provide political and policy cues (Krehbiel 1991). Committees work out both the politics and the policy of a bill and provide key information to each respective body as a whole. Accordingly, a committee's importance can be judged by the quality of information it conveys. In the case of health care, my theory predicts that interest groups should have targeted committees where they had a chance of influencing the ultimate committee outcome as well as the ultimate legislative outcome. The House Education and Labor Committee and the Senate Labor and Human Resources Committee were poor targets because their memberships were not open to persuasion and their decisions were not likely to carry much weight in the Congress as a whole. Consequently, health care bills recommended by committees with liberal majorities would have provided little information to colleagues and the congressional leadership crafting a floor version. As an aide to Majority Leader Mitchell told me, "Kennedy's committee was simply not going to give us enough useful intelligence about the politics of health care."

Legislator Targets

Within the key committees not every member was targeted. As is expected, with a grass roots tactic having a legislative objective, members considered "undecided" or "persuadable" were most likely to be the targets of grass roots lobbying efforts.[4] Table 5.5 reports the individual targets of groups.

Three groups in my sample targeted supporters who needed help explaining their opposition to the Clinton plan to the administration and to the House Democratic leadership. Two groups took advantage of the political environment surrounding the health care situation to build membership. The large majority of groups, however, targeted their grass roots efforts solely at members they considered to be undecided. "Hunt where the ducks

---

[4] Many of the groups I studied utilized more nuanced measures of legislators' predispositions. For instance, many used a one-through-five scale. In cases where I was given more detailed information, I collapsed the five-point scale into a three-point scale, counting soft supporters and opponents as undecided.

Table 5.5. *Legislative Targets within Committee*

Targets	Number of Groups
Supporters	3 (21%)
Opponents	2 (17%)
Undecideds	16 (67%)

Source: Author's interviews.

are," was how one lobbyist explained his tactics to me. He added: "It was good old-fashioned vote counting. We worked with our Hill lobbyists and other allies to determine who was with us and who was against us." Another who was lobbying for the Clinton plan remarked, "We figured out who was for us and who was against us and threw the kitchen sink at everyone in the middle." Pam Bailey of the Healthcare Leadership Council targeted her group efforts to "Specific committees and specific votes" and to "Traditional swing districts" (Stone 1994).

West, Heith, and Goodwin reported the following observations by Bill Gradison, executive director of the HIAA:

We moved our ads around focused on the districts where key committee members were and also on key geographical areas. We felt the battleground would be the Border States and the Southern ones. That's where there were the most conservative Democratic members who we thought would be sympathetic to our message. . . .

We moved around our focus depending on what committee or subcommittee was considering a bill at a particular time. In that sense, it was highly focused. We tried to reach the swing members of those committees on a serial basis depending on when they would be taking things up. (1995, 11, 24)

The nature of my sample, which surely overrepresented large resource-rich groups, clearly affected the influence of organizational factors on lobbying choices. A sample reflecting more accurately all the groups that mobilized around health care would have provided more analytical leverage on the topic of organizational resources and mobilization choices. Still, some speculative assessments on the influence of organizational resources and organizational characteristics on where groups decided to target can be drawn.

On the one hand, trade associations, insurance companies, pharmaceutical companies, and unions all had widespread membership and potential allies virtually everywhere – as well as the money to activate them. Even so, organizational constraints and lack of resources did hamper some groups. For example, a major coalition of pro-reform groups did not have adequate funds and was forced to target many districts with no short-term legislative payoff in an effort to raise money. As an organizer from one of these groups put it: "We were too busy recruiting and trying to keep our heads above water to target effectively. For instance, we had a thousand watch parties when Clinton gave his speech where we had people write their congressman. We tried to spin that in the media as a sign of strength. But it really was a sign of weakness. Most of these people were writing to members who were already with us."

In general, lobbyists trying to mobilize support for health care reform had a tough time. This was the case even for groups with sufficient resources. For example, the American Association of Retired Persons (AARP) and unions were never really able to mobilize the type of support that the administration had expected. According to one administration official, the AARP thought that reform was a done deal and spent too much time trying to fine-tune it. As for the unions, the leadership was supporting the Clinton plan, but the rank and file were skeptical. Most already had good health care plans and had previously sacrificed salary increases to get them. Unions ended up pursuing less focused and less effective campaigns because their membership was not solidly behind them. In addition, unions were left "organizationally exhausted" by their fight against NAFTA.[5]

Another group, the Christian Coalition, used the battle over health care as a recruiting device. Handing out hundreds of thousands of postcards in churches all over the country, it mobilized in many districts whose members already had taken strong positions on the Clinton plan. The postcards they distributed had a Norman Rockwell painting of a mother, child, and doctor. In big letters was the exhortation, "Don't let a government bureaucrat in on this picture." The card then folded out with two preaddressed cards to the worshiper's senators and one to his or her representative. The most important card, though, was the one to be sent back to Christian Coalition headquarters. This card contained the worshiper's name, address, and phone number. This information could then be used for future fund-raising or mobilization campaigns around other issues.

Still, notwithstanding the organizational hurdles that some groups faced and the organization building that some interest groups pursued, the data from interviews with interest groups involved in health care grass roots lobbying are consistent with the theoretical expectations of my model. Interest groups targeted undecided members situated in key legislative positions, where their grass roots lobbying efforts were most likely to make a difference.

---

[5] See Skocpol (1996) for a summary of the major players and their actions during the debate over the Clinton plan.

Constituent Targets

Targeting efforts to stimulate constituent communications is a two-stage process. Once particular districts or states are chosen, particular constituents within those districts need to be identified and mobilized. With a legislative objective, my theory predicts that those with the highest probability of influencing a member of Congress should be the constituents most likely to be targeted. Often, these are constituents with greater resources and more personal connections to a particular member. Yet, they can also be those constituents who possess the credibility to convey particular types of information. Using the data gathered in my interviews, Table 5.6 contains the reports of interest groups on their constituent targets.

Consistent with my expectations about mobilization choices, groups were likely to target those over whom they had leverage (employees and suppliers). For example, IBM, Eastman Kodak, Mobil, DuPont, and Xerox conducted large-scale campaigns to stimulate communications to Congress in targeted districts (Mintz 1994). In-house letters, e-mails, and voice mail messages were some of the tools these companies utilized to contact their employees. Middle management and supervisors were then responsible for follow-up and insuring that contacts were made. One major insurance company targeted all its suppliers and made it known in a not-so-subtle way that each supplier's response would be factored into future purchasing decisions by the company.

Groups also targeted reliable supporters in the form of members and stockholders. Concerned about price caps on prescription drugs, pharmaceutical companies with whom I spoke were especially aggressive about "educating" and targeting stockholders on health care issues. One major pharmaceutical company matched its lists of stockholders and retirees (often large stockholders) to Federal Elections Commission contributor lists and then matched these lists to their correct political geography to determine the "assets" they possessed to influence targeted members of Congress. A group of pharmaceutical companies also conducted focus groups and surveys of stockholders to see which particular messages were most likely to get people to contact their member of Congress about health care legislation.[6] Using their enhanced lists and the messages developed from extensive research, the companies then hired a consulting firm to contact these targeted stockholders. In all, nineteen thousand retired workers and

---

[6] Such research was obviously not unique to the pharmaceutical industry. Virtually every component of the Clinton health care plan was researched with surveys and focus groups. Furthermore, research to gauge the effectiveness of various messages was not only valuable in mobilizing particular constituents but in reframing the issue in general.

Table 5.6. *Constituent Mobilization Targets and Levels of Leverage*

Mobilization Targets	Number of Groups
Members/Stockholders	13
Employees/Vendors	7
Third Party	8
Mixed	7

Source: Author's interviews.

stockholders were patched through to twenty different Congressional offices.[7]

Contacting and recruiting those with a greater probability of influencing a member of Congress were the priorities of many groups. As a government relations official with a pharmaceutical company put it, "When a member of Congress goes home, they spend ninety percent of their time with one percent of the population. We wanted that one percent to be people who were going to communicate our message." The NFIB put in place a program called Guardian Advisory Council (GAC). A GAC team in a targeted congressional district comprised between five and ten influential business people. Along with the more broad-based efforts to mobilize all NFIB members (already an influential group), the GAC teams – composed of larger employers as well as the college friends, neighbors, and former colleagues of the targeted legislator – were also deployed.

Although key contacts were certainly emphasized, there was also a significant level of more broad-based or third-party lobbying campaigns. This is evidenced in Table 5.7, which reports the constituent targets of interest groups.

Yet even these campaigns (in which groups used television or radio advertising to stimulate communications to Congress from constituents outside of their family of members, employers, suppliers, and stockholders) were not shotgun efforts. Particular programs and stations were chosen to maximize the probability that the mobilization requests would not fall on deaf ears, that the correct message would be conveyed, and that the communication would matter. Ben Goddard, who produced and placed the famous

---

[7] Under current lobbying regulations, the company was not required to disclose any of these efforts.

Table 5.7. *Constituent Mobilization Targets*

Mobilization Targets	Number of Groups
Broad Based	15
Key Contacts	11
Mixed	5

Source: Author's interviews.

"Harry and Louise" advertisements for the HIAA, explained, "Our media buys were targeted on involved Americans, people who were registered to vote, wrote letters to editors or public officials, attended meetings and made political contributions.[8] We bought time on CNN and Headline News, CNBC, and Rush Limbaugh" (West et al. 1995, 10).

The Health Insurance Association of America also went for a broader-based strategy because it believed that it needed more credible messengers.[9] An HIAA staff member explained to me, "We were the black hats of the health care game. People like doctors, nurses, and small business. They don't like insurance companies. We needed to work through others to get our message listened to." In its targeted districts the HIAA hired field directors. "These were not just college kids. Our field people had extensive political and public relations experience. Their job was to cultivate allies, gather lists, and find those who would be on our side." The HIAA used a Washington-based consultant to follow through on the responses stimulated by "Harry and Louise" – patch-thrus and telegrams – and relied on their field operatives to stimulate communications from the grass tops.

Both Marty Plisner of CBS News and David Broder of the *Washington Post* pointed out to me that the Republican and antireform groups enjoyed quite an advantage in hiring field operatives. Because the Republicans were out of the White House, there was a real talent pool of Republican campaign and public relations operatives and a lot of highly skilled political people were looking for jobs. For example, the NFIB hired Marc Nuttle, who was the field director for Pat Robertson in his 1988 race for president and is one of the most highly regarded field organizers in GOP circles.[10] On the Demo-

---

[8] Goddard recently married the actress who played Louise.

[9] The actual HIAA lobbying plan was leaked and was widely available in Washington, D.C. It was the subject of numerous media reports, including a lengthy report by Brooks Jackson on CNN (October 19, 1993).

[10] See Kosterlitz (1993) and Weisskopf (1993) for accounts of the scramble for political talent and field operatives in the months preceding the unveiling of the Clinton plan.

cratic side, many of the people with strong field and grass roots experience were enjoying administration jobs.

In short, judgments about the influence, credibility, and direction of a communication appear to have influenced targeting decisions at the individual level. Organizational resources and characteristics, however, also appear to have had a significant influence. Groups made efforts to identify reliable supporters who could influence the legislative process. If they did not have such supporters or if the communications of their reliable supporters would not have been credible – and if they had the monetary resources to do so – they pursued broader-based tactics.

Summary

This overview of mobilization choices made during the legislative battle over health care reform provides confirmatory evidence that mobilization choices were largely a function of group estimates of three characteristics: the persuadability of a legislator, the importance of a legislator, and the influence of citizens. Organizational constraints seem to have influenced the decisions of some lobbyists on the pro-reform side, but the nature of my data makes it difficult to draw any definitive conclusions.

Although the preceding discussion provides a good description of the basic lobbying decisions, my interviews and observations permit me to do more than simply provide descriptive statistics and a basic analysis of tactical choices. Because I gathered more detailed information on the exact targets and messages of groups, I am able to examine in much greater detail the legislators and constituents who were targeted in order to influence the work of three key committees: House Energy and Commerce, House Ways and Means, and Senate Finance.

Energy and Commerce

During the legislative debate over the Clinton plan and health care reform, John Dingell of Michigan chaired the Energy and Commerce Committee. Elected to Congress in 1955 at the age of twenty-nine to succeed his father, Dingell was one of the most senior members of the U.S. House of Representatives. He was a longtime champion of national health care insurance. In fact, at the start of every congressional session, he had made it a habit to submit legislation calling for health coverage for all Americans. When the Democrats controlled Congress, he was considered one of the most powerful committee barons and his committee one of the most powerful. Energy and Commerce handled four out of every ten bills in the House. It had the largest budget and staff of any committee in the House (Barone and Ujifusa 1995).

Furthermore, the Energy and Commerce Committee was considered by lawmakers and lobbyists alike to be representative of the body as a whole and a key cue giver to other members of Congress. "If Commerce couldn't figure this out, nobody could. It was the bellwether committee," explained one business lobbyist. Ira Magaziner, chief of the Clinton health care task force, remarked, "All our political people were telling us that Energy and Commerce was the most important committee – that it most reflected the membership of the House."

In the 103rd Congress, the Energy and Commerce Committee was comprised of twenty-seven Democrats and seventeen Republicans. On health care legislation, initial head counts indicated that Dingell could count on no support at all from Republicans. Thus, he needed the support of twenty-three out of twenty-seven of his Democratic colleagues. My interviews on the Hill, confirmed by contemporaneous media reports, suggested that of those twenty-seven Democrats, Dingell believed he could count on seventeen (*Congressional Quarterly Almanac* 1994). The *Congressional Quarterly Almanac* handicapped the ten remaining Democrats as follows (1994, 335): four members were leaning strongly against the Clinton plan (Ralph Hall of Texas, Billy Tauzin of Louisiana, Roy Rowland of Georgia, and rival-plan author Jim Cooper of Tennessee), three were leaning toward the plan (Lynn Schenk of California, Marjorie Margolies-Mezvinsky of Pennsylvania, and Blanche Lambert of Arkansas), and three were up-for-grabs (Jim Slattery of Kansas, Rick Boucher of Virginia, and Richard Lehman of California).

In Table 5.8, I report three other measures of a member's likelihood of being targeted for a mobilization campaign: the NFIB's handicapping of the Energy and Commerce Committee in the fall of 1993, whether or not a member was a cosponsor of the Clinton plan, and ADA scores. The NFIB system is identical to one that would be used to identify competitive elections or voters in a get-out-the-vote effort: 1 denotes a strong supporter of the Clinton plan; a 2, a member leaning toward the Clinton plan; a 3, a pure undecided; a 4, a member leaning against the Clinton plan; and 5, a strong opponent.

None of these measures is a perfect indicator of a member's predispositions. Cosponsors have been known to change their minds and general ideological scores may say little about attitudes on particular issues. Moreover, the NFIB measure is the assessment of only one group and deals specifically with legislators' predispositions toward the employer mandate in the president's plan. Nevertheless, all else held equal, cosponsors are more likely to support a bill; and ideological scores provide a basic assessment of members' predispositions. In addition, the employer mandate was the main bone of contention in the committee, and the NFIB rankings are virtually identical to targeting assessments that I examined from other groups. In sum, although no individual measure is perfect, to the extent that each indicator points in the same direction, we can be confident in the entire set's utility as a measure of swing legislators.

Given the NFIB estimates, my model of grass roots lobbying decisions predicts that seven Democratic members of the Energy and Commerce Committee should have received the most attention: Representatives Boucher, Cooper, Margolies-Mezvinsky, Lambert, Lehman, Schenk, and Slattery. Moderate members (according to the ADA ratings) Boucher, Cooper, Klug, Lambert, Slattery, Tauzin, and Upton can be judged as likely targets. In addition, we should expect the ten cosponsors of the Clinton plan to have received little or no attention from grass roots lobbyists. (Significantly, none of the previously mentioned legislators was cosponsor.) If we look at a measure of member vulnerability (and thus a need for information on electoral consequences), Representatives Boucher, Cooper, Lambert, Lehman, Margolies-Mezvinsky, Pallone, and Schenk all represented districts that voted for Bush in 1988 and that were barely carried by Clinton in 1992. Rowland and Hall represented districts that were carried by Bush in both 1988 and 1992.

To test how these expectations stacked up against the actual targeting decisions of lobbyists, I asked the representative from each interest group in my study to name the five members on whom they expended the most grass roots lobbying efforts. Of the twenty-one groups with whom I spoke, twenty targeted members of the Energy and Commerce Committee and fifteen were willing or able to give me the breakdown on their mobilization efforts. Their behavior is reported in Table 5.9.

The interview data confirm that swing members of the Energy and Commerce Committee were in fact the ones most likely to be targeted for grass roots mobilization efforts. These data are also consistent with the stylized story that one hears about the fight in the Energy and Commerce Committee. According to the public and private accounts of various interest groups, congressional staffers, White House officials, and members of the press, Chairman Dingell, by April, had managed to convince three of the six undecideds: Representatives Margolies-Mezvinsky, Schenk, and Lambert. At this point, he had twenty votes in hand. Needing three more votes, his attention turned to Representatives Boucher, Lehman, and Slattery. Dingell knew that he needed the support of all three and, as my data demonstrate, so did interest groups.

The tone of the messages used to stimulate constituent communications very much concentrated on short-term direct costs and fears. The following examples illustrate some of the mobilization efforts and advertisements that

Table 5.8. *Handicapping House Energy and Commerce Committee*

Member	NFIB Ratings	Cosponsor	ADA Ratings
Joe Barton, TX-R	5	No	0
Michael Bilirakis, FL-R	5	No	20
Thomas J. Bliley, VA-R	5	No	5
Rick Boucher, VA-D	3	No	60
Sherrod Brown, OH-D	1	Yes	95
John Bryant, TX-D	1	No	90
Cardiss Collins, IL-D	1	Yes	100
Jim Cooper, TN-D	4	No	55
Michael Crapo, ID-R	5	No	5
John D. Dingell, MI-D	1	Yes	70
Jack M. Fields, TX-R	5	No	0
Gary A. Franks, CT-R	5	No	10
Paul E. Gillmor, OH-R	5	No	15
Jim Greenwood, PA-R	5	No	20
Ralph M. Hall, TX-D	4	No	20
Dennis Hastert, IL-R	5	No	5
Scott Klug, WI-R	4	No	40
Mike Kreidler, WA-D	1	Yes	90
Blanche M. Lambert, AR-D	2	No	65
Richard H. Lehman, CA-D	3	No	75
Thomas J. Manton, NY-D	1	No	70

Edward J. Markey, MA-D	1	Yes	95
Alex McMillan, NC-R	5	No	10
Marjorie Margolies-Mezvinsky, PA-D	2	No	80
Carlos J. Moorehead, CA-R	5	No	0
Michael G. Oxley, OH-R	5	No	5
Frank Pallone Jr., NJ-D	2	No	90
Bill Paxon, NY-R	5	No	5
Bill Richardson, NM-D	1	Yes	75
Roy Rowland, GA-D	4	No	20
Dan Schaefer, CO-R	3	No	5
Lynn Schenk, CA-D	2	No	85
Philip R. Sharp, IN-D	1	No	85
Jim Slattery, KS-D	3	No	60
Clifford B. Stearns, FL-R	5	No	15
Gerry E. Studds, MA-D	1	Yes	90
Al Swift, WA-D	1	Yes	95
Michael L. Synar, OK-D	1	Yes	85
J. Tauzin, LA-D	4	No	35
Edolphus Towns, NY-D	1	No	95
Fred Upton, MI-R	4	No	35
Craig Washington, TX-D	1	No	90
Henry A. Waxman, CA-D	1	Yes	100
Ron Wyden, OR-D	1	No	95

Sources: NFIB ratings from author's interviews, ADA ratings from Barone and Ujifusa (1993).

Table 5.9. *Member Targets in House Energy and Commerce Committee*

Member	Groups Mobilizing
Jim Slattery, KS-D	13
Jim Cooper, TN-D	10
Rick Boucher, VA-D	9
Richard H. Lehman, CA-D	9
Lynn Schenk, CA-D	7
Marjorie Margolies-Mezvinsky, PA-D	7
Blanche M. Lambert, AR-D	6
J. Tauzin, CA-D	4
Scott Klug, WI-R	3
Fred Upton, MI-R	2
Ralph M. Hall, TX-D	1
Total	15

Source: Author's interviews.

were used by interest groups to stimulate communications against the Clinton plan in the districts of swing members of the Energy and Commerce Committee.

Citizens for a Sound Economy aired the following radio spot in the districts of Boucher, Lehman, and Slattery.

Announcer: Medical care in America under health care reform [*as telephone rings in background*].
Man: Gatekeeper.
Woman: Hello, this is Mrs. Baylor. My son is having a terrible earache and needs to see Dr. Murray right away.
Man: You will not see Dr. Murray. Dr. Johnson will see your son next week.
Woman: Next week? He needs a doctor now! Is Dr. Johnson an ear specialist?
Man: It doesn't matter.
Woman: Wait a minute. I have health insurance. I don't need you.
Man: Mrs. Baylor, under health reform all Americans – and that includes you and your son – will have to go through government health alliances with gatekeepers like me. We will decide who, when, or even if you see a doctor.
Woman: But this is America!
Announcer: If you don't want government gatekeepers telling you what doctor you can see, call Congressman [name] at [number] and tell him to vote no on the Clinton health care plan. That's [number].

The next example comes from a piece of direct mail aimed at getting small business owners in Richard Lehman's district to contact him. It was sent by the NFIB.

BACK ROOM HEALTH CARE DEAL CUT!
The committee's chairman is working furiously behind closed doors to cut a deal to get Rep. Lehman to support an employer mandate that could be bad for your small business. Call him now at (202) 225-1000 and tell him that the employer mandate will kill jobs and your business.

Interestingly, pro-reform groups were frustrated by the fact that the message that had tested best for them was an anti-Congress one – "you deserve the same health care benefits as Congressman X" – that was killed by a skittish House Democratic leadership. This topic was the subject of much debate among political consultants on the Democratic side. The "every American deserves health care as good as Congress gets" message was eventually used very late in the battle.

Particularly strong attention was paid to Jim Slattery of Kansas. Slattery was running for governor of Kansas and, according to many accounts, was the deciding vote on employer mandates. An action alert sent out by the NFIB by fax and e-mail made the following plea:

Representative Jim Slattery could be the deciding vote on the powerful House Energy and Commerce Committee on the proposal to require you and all small business owners to pay for a government mandated health benefits package for all employees – full time, part time, and seasonal. I need your help to convince him that an employer mandate of any type would be devastating to Kansas small business and your employees. Please call or write to Congressman Jim Slattery today before it's too late! Please do not send a copy of this action alert to Rep. Slattery. Your own letter is much more effective.

Finally, Johnson and Broder (1996) reported the following series of memos from NFIB's House lobbyist Mark Isakowitz to the group's president Jack Faris. They provide an excellent illustration of the sort of tactical logic I have been discussing.

February 12: Rep. Jim Slattery who could be the tie-breaking vote in the Health Subcommittee on the mandate met with Hillary Clinton. Prior to the meeting his staff had told us he had decided to oppose the mandate. After the Hillary meeting, his staff said he was still open to compromise on the mandate. Our latest anti-mandate Action Alert just went out in his district.

March 4: Kim heard from a good source that Rep. Jim Slattery of KS would offer a compromise 50 percent employer mandate in the Commerce Committee. Eight GAC members are going to see him on Monday.

March 11: Eight Kansas GAC members met with Rep. Jim Slattery in Topeka on Monday. He is a key swing vote on Commerce and he told our members he believes there should be some employer mandate in the bill. He is running for governor so there might be some additional grass roots we can do there.

March 25: Rep. Jim Slattery appears to be the major deal maker with Chairman Dingell on this compromise plan. Today, an Action Alert to ALL Kansas NFIB members is going out specifically on Slattery. We are going statewide with the alert because he is running for Governor and has to be sensitive to concerns outside his district. Kim and I met with Slattery on Tuesday.

April 8: The day before Clinton arrived in Topeka to campaign for health care reform
with Rep. Slattery, a group of business owners (including an NFIB member)
unveiled the ad to appear in the next day's Topeka paper announcing the coalition
of more than 1 million employers opposing the mandate.

April 15: Chairman John Dingell continues to negotiate with the people we have been
targeting but does not yet have a majority on the Commerce Committee. There
are signs our grassroots are working. Slattery has retreated some on the mandate,
and is said to have proposed this week a way to get universal coverage without the
mandate; he told our members in March this was impossible.

April 22: Rep. Jim Slattery announced his opposition to the employer mandate
on Thursday saying he was against it and that he wouldn't vote for it even to just
move the process forward in the Commerce Committee. As you know, this is a
complete reversal. We got some credit for it in *The Washington Post* today. (1996,
341–342)

Ultimately, Dingell was not able to convince enough of his Democratic
colleagues. Health care reform never even came to a vote in the Energy and
Commerce Committee. Magaziner lamented, "The NFIB really killed us in
Energy and Commerce. When they won in Dingell's committee, that really
gave heart to our opponents."

Assessments of causality and the granting of credit and blame by the
Washington Post and Magaziner may or may not be accurate. Still, the mobilization decisions made in the Energy and Commerce Committee during the
legislative battle over the Clinton plan and health care reform are an excellent illustration of the careful targeting attention paid to swing members of
key committees. The preceding discussion demonstrated that if we are to
evaluate lobbying influence we need to understand mobilization strategies
and tactics, and the specific political environment in which these decisions
are made. Furthermore, if we are to understand mass participation – if we
are going to understand who participated in Kansas during the battle over
health care reform – we must pay attention to more than personal resources,
attitudes, and attachments.

House Ways and Means Committee

Dan Rostenkowski's Ways and Means Committee was another battleground
in the fight over health care. Although there were many thorny issues, the
central debate revolved around the employer mandate. With Republicans
on the committee unanimously opposed to the employer mandate, Rostenkowski needed the support of twenty out of the twenty-four Democrats
on his committee. Consequently, Rostenkowski worked hard to keep his
members in line and to shield them from constituent pressure. In fact,
after the HIAA's airing of their "Harry and Louise" commercials during

the 1994 February recess unleashed a flood of constituent communications in the districts of some of his key members, Rostenkowski reached an accord with the HIAA to stop agitating the constituents of members of the Ways and Means Committee (Johnson and Broder 1996; Scarlett 1994).

By the time the bill reached markup in the full committee, however, Rostenkowski had been indicted on a series of federal fraud charges and was no longer chairman. The task of shepherding health care reform through the Ways and Means Committee fell to his successor, Representative Sam Gibbons of Florida. There was already a significant amount of attention being paid to the Ways and Means Committee. Nevertheless, according to a number of Hill staffers with whom I spoke, the fall of Rostenkowski made Ways and Means an even more attractive target. Members simply did not owe or fear Chairman Gibbons as much as they had Chairman Rostenkowski. Moreover, with Rostenkowski's demise and Gibbons's ascension, the deals with HIAA and other interest groups broke down, and the "Harry and Louise" commercials started up once again in the districts of swing members of the committee (Johnson and Broder 1996).

The playing field that interest group lobbyists faced is portrayed by the information in Table 5.10. Along with the NFIB ratings, cosponsor status, and ADA scores, I also include whether a member ultimately supported the bill to come out of committee. To judge from the NFIB scores, Michael Andrews of Texas, Bill Brewster of Oklahoma, Peter Hoagland of Nebraska, and L. F. Payne of Virginia should have been prime targets. Looking at ADA scores, Andrews, Brewster, Hoagland, Payne, J. J. Pickle of Texas, and Nancy Johnson of Connecticut should have been the focus of mobilization efforts. The eight cosponsors of the Clinton plan should not be expected to have received much attention. (None of the names previously mentioned as targets were cosponsors.) Andrews can be excluded from the list because information on the electoral consequences of health care reform was of no use to him. He had lost a March race for the Democratic Senate nomination in Texas and was not running for reelection to the House. Similarly, Pickle was retiring and was not likely to be susceptible to mobilization pressure or in need of the information that it provided. In sum, three names come up in all the measures: Brewster, Hoagland, and Payne. Hoagland and Payne represented districts won by Bush in both 1988 and 1992. Brewster's district was won by Bush in 1988 and only narrowly carried by Clinton in 1992.

Fifteen groups with whom I spoke targeted the Ways and Means Committee and thirteen of these groups were willing and able to provide me with

Table 5.10. *Handicapping House Ways and Means Committee*

Member	NFIB Ratings	Cosponsor	ADA Ratings	Actual Vote
Michael A. Andrews, TX-D	3	No	55	No
Bill Archer, TX-R	5	No	5	No
Bill Brewster, OK-D	3	No	25	No
Jim Bunning, KY-R	5	No	10	No
Dave Camp, MI-R	5	No	5	No
Benjamin L. Cardin, MD-D	1	Yes	90	Yes
William J. Coyne, PA-D	5	Yes	95	No
Philip M. Crane, IL-R	5	No	15	No
Harold E. Ford, TN-D	1	No	80	Yes
Sam M. Gibbons, FL-D	1	No	75	Yes
Fred Grandy, IA-R	4	No	20	No
Mel Hancock, MO-R	5	No	5	No
Wally Herger, CA-R	5	No	5	No
Peter Hoagland, NE-D	3	No	65	No
Amo Houghton, NY-R	4	No	20	No
Andy Jacobs Jr., IN-D	1	No	90	Yes
William J. Jefferson, CA-D	2	No	95	Yes

Name	NFIG	Cosponsor	ADA	Vote
Nancy L. Johnson, CT-R	4	No	40	No
Barbara B. Kennelly, CT-D	2	No	90	Yes
Gerald D. Kleczka, WI-D	1	No	80	Yes
Mike Kopetski, OR-D	1	No	85	Yes
Sander M. Levin, MI-D	1	Yes	95	Yes
John Lewis, GA-D	5	No	100	Yes
Robert T. Matsui, CA-D	1	Yes	80	Yes
Jim McCrery, LA-R	5	No	0	No
Jim McDermott, WA-D	1	No	85	No
Michael R. McNulty, NY-D	2	No	60	Yes
Richard E. Neal, MA-D	2	No	95	Yes
L. F. Payne, VA-D	3	No	30	Yes
J. J. Pickle, TX-D	1	No	65	Yes
Charles B. Rangel, NY-D	1	Yes	95	Yes
Mel Reynolds, IL-D	1	Yes	90	Yes
Dan Rostenkowski, IL-D	1	Yes	90	Yes
Rick Santorum, PA-R	5	No	20	No
E. Clay Shaw, Jr., FL-R	5	No	10	No
Fortney H. Stark, CA-D	1	Yes	100	Yes
Don Sundquist, TN-R	5	No	5	No
William M. Thomas, CA-R	5	No	5	No

Sources: NFIG ratings from author's interviews, ADA ratings from Barone and Ujifusa (1993). Cosponsor and vote in committee come from Legislate on-line service.

Table 5.11. *Member Targets in House Ways and Means Committee*

Member	Groups Mobilizing
Peter Hoagland, NE-D	12
Bill Brewster, OK-D	10
L. F. Payne, VA-D	10
William J. Jefferson, CA-D	6
Richard E. Neal, MA-D	3
Barbara B. Kennelly, CT-D	3
Nancy L. Johnson, CT-R	2
Sander M. Levin, MI-D	2
Michael A. Andrews, TX-D	2
Total	13

Source: Author's interviews.

targeting information. Table 5.11 shows the individual targets of groups using mobilization tactics in the Ways and Means Committee.

Again, the findings are consistent with theoretical expectations. Hoagland, Brewster, and Payne – who by multiple indicators were the swing votes on Ways and Means and the most in need of information on the political consequences of their actions – were the members most likely to be targeted by grass roots lobbyists. They were on the receiving end of advertisements like the ones I outlined in the previous section on the Energy and Commerce Committee. William Jefferson of Louisiana was also the focus of significant lobbying attention. Although African American and generally considered a liberal member of Congress, he was not a cosponsor of the Clinton plan and had aspirations to run in a statewide race for governor. He was also an active member of the Democratic Leadership Council. Connecticut members Barbara Kennelly and Nancy Johnson (the only Republican on the list) as well as Richard Neal of Massachusetts were targeted by home district insurance companies.

The Ways and Means Committee eventually reported out a bill by a two-vote margin (20 to 18). No Republicans voted in favor of the legislation. Of the three members who received the most grass roots lobbying attention, Hoagland and Brewster voted "no" and Payne voted "yes." Jim McDermott, a liberal Democrat from Washington state and a strong proponent of the single-payer option, voted against the Ways and Means version because he felt it did not go far enough toward providing universal health care coverage for all Americans (Clymer, Pear, and Toner 1994).

The Senate Finance Committee and the Mainstream Coalition

The Finance Committee in the Senate was perceived in very much the same way as the Energy and Commerce Committee was in the House. The *Congressional Quarterly Almanac* commented, "The Senate Finance Committee occupied a pivotal place in the health care debate. Many lawmakers, especially in the House, were counting on the panel to craft a grand compromise that could attract votes from both parties and pave the way for skittish members to vote for an overhaul bill" (1994, 338).

Daniel Patrick Moynihan of New York chaired the Finance Committee. Faced with a slim eleven to nine Democratic advantage in his committee, Moynihan could not afford to lose even a single Democrat if he was to report out legislation. Moreover, other accounts indicated that Moynihan was opposed to the strategy of just getting the legislation through with Democratic votes. He knew that the real goal was sixty votes in the Senate and wanted to craft a bill that would attract enough Republican votes to avert a filibuster. Furthermore, although Democrats enjoyed only a slim majority in the committee, the atmosphere was less partisan than in the House and there were moderate Republicans with whom Moynihan hoped to work.

Table 5.12 depicts measures of members' predispositions in the Senate Finance Committee.

According to NFIB estimates, Senators Max Baucus of Montana, David Boren of Oklahoma, John Breaux of Louisiana, and Kent Conrad of North Dakota should have drawn the most attention of grass roots lobbyists. Senators Bill Bradley of New Jersey, John Danforth of Missouri, Dave Durenberger of Minnesota, and John Chafee of Rhode Island were also potential targets according to the NFIB. ADA scores point in the direction of Senators Breaux (who was also very active in the Democratic Leadership Council), Chafee, Danforth, Durenberger, Bob Packwood of Oregon, and Bill Roth of Delaware. Although both Durenberger's and Danforth's ADA scores and NFIB projections suggested that they could have been likely targets, neither was running for reelection and therefore did not need information on the electoral consequences of their actions. Because of Packwood's problems with the ethics committee and his reliance on the Republican leadership for protection, conventional wisdom was that Minority Leader Bob Dole essentially controlled his vote. Although Baucus and Conrad were cosponsors of the Clinton plan, both had publicly expressed strong reservations about the employer mandate (Johnson and Broder 1996).

Table 5.12. *Handicapping Senate Finance Committee*

Member	NFIB Ratings	Cosponsor	ADA Ratings	Actual Vote
Max Baucus, MI-D	3	Yes	85	Yes
David Lyle Boren, OK-D	3	No	70	Yes
Bill Bradley, NJ-D	2	No	90	Yes
John B. Breaux, LA-D	3	No	40	Yes
John H. Chafee, RI-R	4	No	55	Yes
Kent Conrad, ND-D	3	Yes	80	No
John C. Danforth, MO-R	4	No	35	Yes
Thomas A. Daschle, SD-D	1	Yes	35	Yes
Robert Dole, KS-R	5	No	10	No
Dave Durenberger, MN-R	4	No	75	No
Charles E. Grassley, IA-R	5	No	20	No
Orrin G. Hatch, UT-R	5	No	5	No
George J. Mitchell, ME-D	1	Yes	85	Yes
Daniel Patrick Moynihan, NY-D	1	Yes	90	Yes
Bob Packwood, OR-R	5	No	35	No
David Pryor, AR-D	1	Yes	70	Yes
Donald W. Riegle Jr., MI-D	1	Yes	80	Yes
John D. Rockefeller IV, WV-D	1	Yes	70	Yes
William V. Roth Jr., DE-R	5	No	45	No
Malcolm Wallop, WY-R	5	No	5	No

Sources: NFIB ratings from author's interviews, ADA ratings from Barone and Ujifusa (1993). Cosponsor and vote in committee come from Legislate on-line service.

Table 5.13. *Member Targets in Senate Finance Committee*

Senator	Number of Groups Mobilizing
John Breaux, LA-D	11
Max Baucus, MI-D	9
Kent Conrad, ND-D	8
John Chafee, RI-R	8
David Boren, OK-D	5
Bill Bradley, NJ-D	5
Daniel Patrick Moynihan, NY-D	3
Total	13

Source: Author's interviews.

Chafee and Breaux were considered two especially important targets because of their influence with two important Senate constituencies: moderate Republicans and conservative Democrats.

Table 5.13 reports targeting choices of interest groups. Of the sixteen groups who targeted the Finance Committee, targeting information was available from thirteen.

Once again, the actual targeting decisions were consistent with expectations. The undecided and influential were more likely to be targeted by groups attempting to stimulate constituent communications to Congress. In addition, consistent with the general notion that groups employing grass roots tactics with a legislative objective should target their efforts where they have the greatest probability of making a difference, many groups pursued a small-state strategy. As one lobbyist put it, "fifty small businessmen are going to influence Max [Baucus] in Montana a lot more than fifty small businessmen are going to influence Moynihan in Manhattan." In other words, the lower the denominator – the fewer constituents – the higher the probability that any one communication would make a difference. Similarly, advertising time was cheaper in Montana and other small cities.

Also, in the Senate, a group known as the mainstream coalition – or the rump group – comprised a virtual sixth committee dealing with health care legislation. Comprised of conservative Democrats and moderate Republicans in the Senate, and under the tutelage of Senator Chafee (also a member of Senate Finance) the mainstream coalition worked to forge a compromise plan. Unofficial members included Republicans Durenberger, Danforth, and Mark Hatfield of Oregon as well as Democrats Joseph Lieberman of Connecticut, Sam Nunn of Georgia, Byron Dorgan of North Dakota, Frank

Lautenberg of New Jersey, J. Bennett Johnston Jr. of Louisiana, and Bob Kerrey and James Exon of Nebraska (Clymer et al. 1994; *Congressional Quarterly Almanac* 1994, 351; Johnson and Broder 1996).

These senators held the key to breaking a filibuster (Brady and Buckley 1995). Moreover, many of them were considered cue givers. For instance, Sam Nunn's major area was defense issues, but he was also very influential with conservative southern Democrats. Laurie Sullivan, an Aetna vice-president, described her company's rationale for targeting Lieberman: "His network of contacts gives him greater influence than many other senators" (quoted in McDonald 1994). Although my data do not permit me to measure the level of interest group attention to this other virtual committee, comments and media accounts indicate that there was significant grass roots attention paid to the rump group.

Chapter Summary

In 1993 and 1994 millions of Americans communicated their feelings about health care to Congress. This chapter has demonstrated that to understand why people contacted Congress and what influence these contacts had, we must understand the elite decisions driving much of this participation. In short, this chapter has demonstrated that whether we want to understand mass participation or interest group influence, we must understand how institutional and political forces structure lobbying choices. In the battle over health care reform, demographics and attitudes alone did not determine who participated, and PAC donations and inside lobbying were not the only ways that organized interests attempted to influence the process.

The predominant strategic objective of interest groups pursuing grass roots tactics in the battle over health care reform was to influence the current legislative battle by demonstrating constituent opinion and by establishing traceability. Given this objective, the choices and decisions around health care were consistent with the theoretical expectations outlined in Chapter 3. Admittedly, my data do not comprise a representative sample of all choices surrounding health care lobbying. Still, a diverse set of evidence demonstrated that interest groups carefully targeted their grass roots efforts at the districts of persuadable legislators on key committees and at influential members in the Congress as a whole. Within these chosen districts, employees, customers, suppliers, and stockholders were targeted with messages that accentuated the short-term costs of health care reform.

To reiterate, I am not suggesting that there were not other objectives – mobilizing and/or rewarding friends, for example – or that other members of committees and other members of Congress were not the targets of other types of lobbying. Consistent with my framework of lobbying, interest groups possess multiple motives and multiple ways of achieving their goals. Interest groups may well have been trying to get supporters to the table and/ or encouraging them to work harder once there.

For example, the top five recipients of contributions from PACs with an interest in health care were John Dingell ($170,460), Marjorie Margolies-Mezvinsky ($143,860), Lynn Schenk ($111,524), Thomas Bliley ($104,950), and Craig Washington ($98,100). The targeting patterns of these contributions were not the same as the targeting choices for grass roots campaigns. Yet, these data are not a competing piece of evidence. Instead, they demonstrate that scholars striving to understand interest group tactics must understand how tactics are influenced by strategic objectives and must be precise about what these strategic objectives are.

Finally, since observations and interviews demonstrated that interest groups mobilized in expected ways during the battle over health care, the logical next question is whether these mobilization decisions filtered through to the mass public. Is there evidence that mobilization mattered and that it was pursued in the expected places? In the next chapter, in an effort to answer this question, I combine the information I gathered on targets in this chapter with two national public opinion surveys conducted during the summer of 1994.

6

Patterns of Recruitment and Participation in the Mass Public

In the previous chapter, I used formal interviews, media accounts, and my own observations to gather information from the top down on the lobbying choices and targeting decisions of interest groups in the battle over health care reform. Consistent with theoretical expectations, the evidence revealed that the legislative targets in grass roots campaigns on health care were likely to be undecideds, key committee members, and cue givers. Greater variation existed among constituency targets – with some groups concentrating on members, employees, and stockholders, while other groups pursued more broad-based tactics. Still, the evidence indicated that lobbyists targeted more engaged and influential constituents who could be counted on to deliver the correct messages.

In this chapter, I investigate from the bottom up the impact of these decisions at the mass level. I investigate whether there is evidence among the mass public to confirm the reports of lobbyists and support my model of mobilization choices. Were citizens residing in states represented by undecideds and cue givers on key committees more likely to be contacted by interest groups? Were more educated and wealthy citizens more likely to be contacted? Were contacted citizens and those living in targeted districts and states more likely to get in touch with Congress about health care legislation or the Clinton plan?

The fundamental approach in this chapter is to add contextual information about targeted districts to individual-level survey data containing measures of participation and mobilization.[1] This method allows me to vary the strategic situation and gauge how the political environment surrounding health care influenced both elite mobilization and citizen participation. The

---

[1] I had also hoped to merge data on targeted districts with information on patterns of incoming communications from individual legislator's offices. However, as discussed in more detail in Appendix B, low response rates to the congressional communications survey I conducted and concerns about the reliability and validity of the data precluded me from using it for more in-depth analysis.

106

information on targeted states and districts comes from the research reported in Chapter 5. The survey data come from two national surveys conducted during the summer of 1994.

Stimulating Participation in Targeted States

First, I use a 1994 Battleground Poll to study the direct effect of recruitment contacts and to examine recruitment patterns for health care reform lobbying directed toward the Senate (see Appendix A). The Battleground Poll was conducted during August 1994. It questioned a national sample of one thousand registered voters and comprised a joint effort between two Washington, D.C., polling firms: a Democratic firm, Mellman-Lazarus-Lake, and a Republican firm, The Tarrance Group.

Admittedly, the Battleground Poll is not ideal for scholarly purposes. It only questioned registered voters who, by definition, have a predisposition toward participating in politics. It also had a short field-period of only four days, raising questions of nonresponse bias. Moreover, the "communicating to Congress on health care" question was asked of only half the sample. And finally, interest group affiliations as well as certain useful demographic and attitudinal questions such as church attendance, religion, and political efficacy were not included.

Nevertheless, callback procedures were followed, professional, well-trained interviewers were used, and extensive monitoring was employed. It was also one of the few surveys to include questions about communications to Congress during the battle over health care reform. Furthermore, it is the only 1994 survey of which I am aware that asked questions about being recruited to communicate with Congress and about communications to Congress on the specific issue of health care. The instrumentation on health care-related participation allows me to combine these data with information on the legislative targets I gathered and reported in Chapter 5.

The Model

As discussed in much greater detail in the preceding chapter, the main targets for players in the health care battle were undecided members of three key committees – Senate Finance, House Ways and Means, and House Energy and Commerce. In addition, a group of moderate senators, dubbed "the rump group," comprised a virtual fourth targeted committee and were also the focus of grass roots mobilization campaigns. Although health care legislation was debated in two other committees, neither opponents nor proponents of the Clinton health care plan paid much attention to the Senate Labor and Human Resources Committee and the House Education

Table 6.1. *Targeted States*

States	Senators
Connecticut	Joseph Lieberman (D)
Georgia	Sam Nunn (D)
Louisiana	John Breaux (D) *, J. Bennet Johnston Jr. (D)
Montana	Max Baucus (D) *
Nebraska	Bob Kerrey (D), James Exon (D)
New Jersey	Bill Bradley (D) *, Frank Lautenberg(D)
North Dakota	Kent Conrad (D) *, Byron Dorgan (D)
Oklahoma	David Boren (D) *
Rhode Island	John Chafee (R) *
Tennessee	Rep. Jim Cooper (D)
Kansas	Rep. Jim Slattery (D)

* Member of Senate Finance Committee.
Source: Author's compilation. See text.

and Labor Committee. Both of these committees had strong liberal majorities and were unlikely to provide much useful information and political
intelligence to their respective bodies.

There were indications of other grass roots campaigns directed toward
undecided members in the full bodies. Nevertheless, in both houses, the
major focus of mobilization efforts was at the committee level. Unfortunately, the Battleground Poll only recorded the state of each respondent and
not his or her Congressional district. Therefore, I was only able to combine
the Battleground data with information on targeted senators and targeted
states. In the following section of this chapter, I use a Times-Mirror poll to
examine participation patterns in the House (see Appendix A).

The data from my elite interviews revealed that nine states were targeted
for grass roots mobilization campaigns around health care. Extensive statewide mobilization campaigns were also conducted in Kansas, where Representative Jim Slattery was running for governor, and in Tennessee, where
Representative Jim Cooper was running for the Senate. The full list of
targeted states is contained in Table 6.1.

There was not a sufficient number of respondents in the Battleground
Poll to examine behavior in the individual states. But the responses of residents of targeted states can be combined to provide a contextual variable
that measures a similar political environment. As described in more detail in
the previous chapter, this atmosphere was characterized by extensive radio
and television media campaigns, mailings, organized town meetings, profes-

sional phone banks, and grass roots campaigns run by full-time state organizers. Accordingly, the survey question on whether a respondent was personally urged to participate measures direct mobilization. The targeted state variable measures other indirect mobilization influences and the effect of being in a competitive political environment.

In addition to being contacted by a group and living in a targeted state, I also include other common correlates of participation that should be a part of any well-specified model of communicating with Congress.[2] These include age, race, education, marital status, employment status, self-described class, and party identification. (See Appendix A for a description of question wordings and codings.)

I present these data in both bivariate and multicausal form. For the multicausal case I estimate my models with logit regression. Due to the dichotomous nature of the dependent variable, logit regression makes good methodological sense and has often been used when models of participation are estimated. Logit regression makes good theoretical sense as well. We should not expect mobilization to mean the same thing to different people at different times. Mobilization should mean the most to those on the cusp – and this is precisely what the S-curve of the logit estimator assumes.

To gauge the independent influence of living in a targeted state on being recruited by a group or lobbying firm, I also model the process by which citizens are asked to communicate to Congress. Unfortunately, although the Battleground Poll did ask if respondent were mobilized to contact Congress, it does not ask what they were mobilized about or who mobilized them. Consequently, the dependent variable in this model is measuring general mobilization, while the contextual independent variable measures the political environment just about health care. Nevertheless, with the enormous attention and resources paid to the targeted legislators in the battle over health care, even with this source of measurement error, we still should expect to find evidence that the political environment surrounding health care reform influenced even general patterns of mobilization.

Results

According to the Battleground Poll, one in five registered voters (20 percent) reported that he or she had communicated with a member of Congress about health care in the past year, and more than four in ten (43 percent)

---

[2] As noted previously, the survey did not contain many of the questions that scholars commonly have used in modeling participation – church attendance, efficacy, length of residence, political knowledge, media habits, or home ownership. In modeling the likelihood of being mobilized it would also have been useful to have some measure of interest group membership. Still, even though recruitment of members is a common tactic, organized interests often cast their net in a wider fashion as well.

Table 6.2. *Personal Characteristics and Communicating with Congress on Health Care*

Higher Than Average Levels of Contacting	Lower Than Average Levels of Contacting
White: 21%	Black: 15%
Age 65 and Over: 30%	Age 18–34: 11%
College Grad: 30%	High School Grad: 13%
Republican: 22%	Democrat: 18%
Upper Class: 38%	Working Class: 13%
Working: 25%	Not Working: 17%
Married: 25%	Nonmarried: 12%
Mobilized: 36%	Not Mobilized: 10%
Targeted State 32%	Nontargeted State 18%

Note: N = 500. For codings and question wordings, see appendix A.
Source: Battleground Poll, August 1994.

reported that they had been mobilized. As I noted before, the mobilization question did not ask on what issue a respondent was mobilized. Also, a little over one-third (34 percent) of registered voters in the Battleground Poll reported they had telephoned, faxed, or sent a letter in the past year on any topic. Table 6.2 provides more information on exactly who was likely to convey their opinions on health care issues to Congress.

Consistent with previous studies of participation, those more likely to contact Congress were the more educated, the employed, the married, and the wealthy. It was also the case that Republicans were more likely to communicate their feelings on health care to their representatives in Washington. (More on this point later in the chapter.) In addition, there was a slight racial gap, with blacks less likely to voice their feelings about health care than whites.

Interestingly, members of union households communicated on the health care issue at exactly the same rate as the population as a whole. This was not the case with communications to Congress in general, where members of union households out-participated nonunion households by 16 percentage points (41 percent to 25 percent). This finding is consistent with what I was told in my interviews – that unions had exhausted most of their time and resources on NAFTA and never became a player in the battle over health care.[3]

---

[3] I should note that one union official whom I interviewed angrily denied the claim that unions never showed up for the battle over health care.

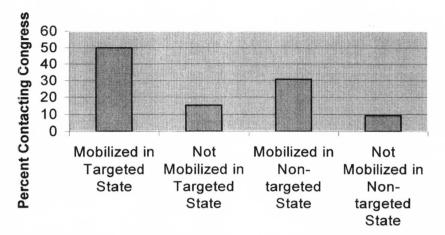

Figure 6.1. Mobilization and participation in target and nontarget states (n = 1,000). For coding and question wordings, see Appendix A. *Source:* Battleground Poll, August 1994.

Moving to the main topic of interest, respondents who resided in any of the eleven states targeted for statewide grass roots campaigns in the battle over health care had a participation rate 14 percentage points higher than those in other states (32 percent to 18 percent). Looking at the effect of direct mobilization on communications to Congress about health care, more than one-third (36 percent) of those who claimed a mobilization contact reported communicating to one of their senators or representatives in Washington about health care. In sharp contrast, only one in ten (10 percent) of noncontacted respondents reported such communication.

Figure 6.1 combines information about direct recruitment and the political environment. Specifically, it illustrates the participation rates for mobilized and nonmobilized respondents in targeted and nontargeted states.

As the bar chart in Figure 6.1 illustrates, citizens receiving a recruitment contact in targeted states were more likely to participate than citizens receiving a recruitment contact in nontargeted states. Similarly, albeit at a much lower level, citizens receiving a recruitment contact in nontargeted states were more likely to contact Congress than noncontacted citizens in nontargeted states. Not surprisingly, citizens receiving a recruitment contact in targeted states had the highest level of contacting Congress (50 percent).

Looking at the effect of recruitment activities in yet a different way, almost three in four persons who contacted Congress about health care legislation (72 percent) reported that they had been asked to do so. Table 6.3 illustrates exactly which citizens were likely to receive a mobilization contact. Even

Table 6.3. *Personal Characteristics and Being Mobilized to Contact Congress*

Higher Than Average Levels of Mobilization	Lower Than Average Levels of Mobilization
White: 45%	Black: 22%
Male: 46%	Female: 39%
Age 65 and over: 46%	Age 18–34: 29%
College Grad: 55%	High School Grad: 30%
Married: 46%	Nonmarried: 38%
Working: 25%	Not Working: 17%
Union Household: 51%	Nonunion Household: 41%
Upper Class: 50%	Working Class: 22%
Republican: 44%	Democrat: 40%
Target State: 50%	Nontargeted State: 40%

Notes: N = 1,000. For codings and question wordings, see Appendix A.
Source: Battleground Poll, August 1994.

using this broad measure of recruitment, respondents in the eleven states targeted for health care lobbying were more likely to receive a request to participate. Also, as expected, the educated and the self-described upper class were more likely to have received a recruitment contact. Furthermore, there was a slight gender gap, with men more likely to receive a request than women. Republicans were also slightly more likely to be recruited than Democrats.

So far, at least in the bivariate case, there is evidence that elite efforts mattered and that lobbyists targeted influential constituents to communicate with influential members of Congress.

Before presenting the results of the logit regression, I must address a tricky theoretical and statistical problem extant in studying the effect of recruitment contacts on participation. Put simply, do recruitment efforts cause citizens to participate, or are citizens targeted because they are likely to participate in the first place? Statistically speaking, in determining the effect of a mobilization contact, there is a selection bias due to nonrandom assignment. Such a problem arises when methods assume a random assignment to different treatment groups when, in reality, this is not the case. A model that wrongly assumes a random assignment will yield a stochastic component with an expected value not equal to zero.

Since the point of this project is to argue that elite lobbying decisions are far from random and have a unique political logic, this is clearly a potential

Table 6.4. *Causes of Phoning, Faxing, or Writing Congress on Health Care*

Variable	Coefficient	Standard Error	Partial Effect
White	−.21	.37	
Male	−.01	.25	
Under 35	−.78	.49	
Over 65	.73	.30	8
Education	1.14	.43	13
Strong Partisan	.05	.29	
Union Household	.15	.32	
Employed	.70	.22	8
Upper Class	.98	.38	11
Republican	.33	.22	
Married	.80	.29	10
Targeted State and Not Mobilized	.77	.33	9
Mobilized	1.40	.25	20

Notes: N = 500. Percentage of cases correctly predicted = 82% (null mode = 80%). For codings and question wordings, see Appendix A.
Source: Battleground Poll, August 1994.

problem. In fact, part of the logic of my theoretical model is that citizens are being contacted for a reason that is tied to their probability of participating. In practice, however, I think the consequences for my estimates are quite small. My model already includes many of the factors that lobbyists might employ in making their recruitment choices. Also, the sample comprised registered voters who were reachable in a four-day period by phone. These are precisely the types of citizens that lobbyists are likely to target – and are likely to be able to target. These conditions may bias in an upward fashion the logit coefficient measuring mobilization contacts (the effect of mobilization might not be so high for the general public). But it also lessens the chance that a coefficient might be biased due to nonrandom selection. Moreover, it is unlikely that interest groups targeted whole states with a predisposition to participate and that those states precisely matched my set of lobbying targets.

The findings from the bivariate analysis are confirmed when a logit model is used to sort out individual effects. The results of the model are reported in Table 6.4. In addition to the coefficients and standard errors, for those coefficients that were statistically significant at the commonly used 95 per-

Table 6.5. *Causes of Being Mobilized*

Variable	Coefficient	Standard Error	Partial Effect
White	.27	.19	
Male	.28	.14	7
Under 35	−.76	.22	−15
Over 65	.32	.17	
Education	1.48	.23	30
Strong Partisan	−.06	.18	
Employed	.28	.13	7
Upper Class	1.35	.26	27
Republican	.34	.29	
Union Household	.40	.17	9
Married	.16	.15	
Targeted State	.48	.20	11

Notes: N = 1,000. Percentage of cases correctly predicted = 64% (null model = 57%). For codings and question wordings, see Appendix A.
Source: Battleground Poll, August 1994.

cent confidence level, I also report the partial effects of independent variables (in percentage points) on the probability of communicating with Congress. For each of the variables, I calculated the probability that each respondent would communicate to Congress under two scenarios, assuming that the variable takes its lowest value and then assuming that it takes its highest value, allowing all other variables to take their observed values. The reported effect is the difference between the two probabilities averaged across the entire sample.

With other factors held constant, recruitment still had a large effect on participation rates. Directly recruited individuals were 20 percentage points more likely to communicate to Congress than those who were not contacted by an interest group.

Looking at the individual attributes that influenced who was contacted, Table 6.5 reports the results of a model in which being asked to communicate with Congress was the dependent variable. With other influences held constant, we see that whites, males, and the better educated were significantly more likely to receive a request. Younger voters were less likely to be targeted for recruitment.

This analysis provides more evidence that lobbyists targeted individuals for whom mobilization would make a difference in their decision to participate as well as individuals whose communications would be influential. Most importantly, we also have further confirmation that citizens who resided in states represented by influential senators were more likely to be targeted for a contact. With all else held constant, a resident of a targeted state was 11 percentage points more likely to be targeted.

Because of their organizational affiliation, members of union households were more likely to be contacted. As discussed previously, however, unions never really came to the fight in the battle over the Clinton health care plan. Although members of union households were more likely to receive a general recruitment contact, they were no more likely to contact their legislators on health care legislation. But, on the general communicating to Congress question, by a margin of 41 percent to 31 percent, members of union households were more likely to communicate with Congress. This finding holds up in a multicausal model as well (Goldstein 1995).

To examine further the characteristics of constituents targeted for mobilization, I calculated a set of representation ratios. A representation ratio measures how underrepresented or overrepresented a particular group is relative to its share of the total population. For example, if college-educated citizens comprise 20 percent of the potential electorate and 30 percent of the actual electorate their representation ratio would be 1.50. Likewise, if lower-income individuals comprise 30 percent of the potential electorate but only 15 percent of actual voters, their representation ratio would be .50 (see Rosenstone and Hansen 1993).

As Table 6.6 illustrates, the focus of lobbyists on higher-end constituents is also demonstrated by the preceding representation ratios. They show that college graduates and the self-described upper class were contacted by groups at a rate greater than the proportion they composed in the population as a whole. In general, these findings about recruitment patterns and citizen communications to Congress underscore the fact that grass roots lobbying tactics create multiple biases in favor of those with greater resources. Those with greater resources and skills are not only more likely to have the ability to communicate with Congress in the first place, but are also more likely to be contacted by elites. Further, their participation is likely to count more with members of Congress.

To sum up, according to the Battleground Poll, recruitment had a statistically and substantively large influence on individuals' likelihoods of contacting Congress on health care. Even with all the national attention paid to the issue and the personal stake that every American had in the legislation, citizens still needed a push to participate. Moreover, there was evidence at the individual level that lobbyists systematically targeted their efforts where they were most likely to influence the ultimate outcome. Residents of states with undecided or influential senators on key committees were more likely

Table 6.6. *Representation Ratios for Being Mobilized*

Subgroup	Representation Ratio
Education	
Less than High School	.7
High School	.75
Some College	1.03
College Grad	1.28
Class	
Working Class	.72
Lower Class	.78
Middle Class	1.10
Upper Class	1.65

Note: N = 1,000.
Source: Battleground Poll, August 1994.

to be targeted and were more likely to contact Congress. Also, there was evidence that organized interests targeted their recruitment efforts toward those who were likely to respond and whose contact would have an influence. Respondents with higher resources and more influence were more likely to be contacted and were more likely to communicate with Congress. In short, the behavior reported in the Battleground Poll is consistent with the theoretical expectations outlined in Chapter 3 and the empirical findings regarding interest group recruitment choices reported in Chapter 5.

Mobilization and Targeted House Districts

Turning to another data set, I use a July 1994 Times-Mirror poll to examine participation focused on the House (see Appendix A). The study does not have self-representing samples of congressional districts. Still, the large number of respondents (3,800 voting-age population) ensures an adequate representation when House districts with similar political environments are aggregated.[4]

[4] The Times-Mirror Poll does not ascertain the congressional district of respondents. However, the staff at the Times-Mirror Center for the People and the Press (now the Pew Center) provided me with the telephone numbers of respondents. With the phone numbers, I worked with Survey Sampling, a Connecticut-based sampling company, to match the area codes and exchanges to particular congressional districts. Because of some overlap with exchanges and congressional districts, this process was not perfect. In the 11 percent of the cases where exchanges overlapped districts, the district where the majority of the exchange was located was selected. There is no reason to believe that this introduced any sort of systematic bias.

Although the Times-Mirror questionnaire contains more of the variables that should be correlated with participation (political information, church attendance, efficacy, and media usage) than does the contemporaneous Battleground Poll, it does not ask whether respondents were recruited and does not ask respondents why they contacted Congress. These omissions pose serious problems. For instance, the lack of a question on recruitment makes it impossible to examine the direct effect of a recruitment contact. Furthermore, since different legislators and Congressional districts were in play with different issues, not knowing which issue spurred a respondent to contact his or her legislator makes it difficult to add contextual data on the political environment in the district.

Nonetheless, enormous attention was paid to lobbying over health care. Even using a general measure of participation, we should still expect to find higher rates of participation in targeted districts. Furthermore, since there was a major push to spur constituent communications on health care in the spring of 1994, a general question asked immediately after a flurry of mobilization activity on health care in July 1994 should pick up variations in areas targeted. Therefore, even though the Times-Mirror poll did not measure all the different types of grass roots campaigns that were conducted, the district targeting variable I constructed used the information on House targets in the battle over health care reform that I gathered from my interviews dealing with health care reform.

The roster of targeted members and districts is presented in Table 6.7. The targeted districts are the ones that were represented by swing members of the House Energy and Commerce Committee as well as the House Ways and Means Committee. The information comes from the empirical work reported in Chapter 5.

In modeling contacting Congress, I included the following additional variables: age, race, sex, education level, employment status, member of a union household, marital status, home ownership, church attendance, strength of partisanship, party identification, political knowledge, political efficacy, and media habits. Again, I present the data in both bivariate and multicausal form and estimate my multicausal model with logit.

Results

A little over one-quarter (28 percent) of respondents to the July 1994 Times-Mirror Poll reported that they had contacted their senator or representative in Washington during the past year. Table 6.8 provides the bivariate breakdown of those who reported communicating to Congress in the past year.

Again, consistent with the Battleground Poll's findings on health care participation and scores of previous studies on the correlates of participa-

Table 6.7. *Targeted House Districts*

Member	Party	State and District
Slattery	Democrat	KS-2
Cooper	Democrat	TN-4
Boucher	Democrat	VA-9
Lehman	Democrat	CA-19
Schenk	Democrat	CA-49
Margolies-Mezvinsky	Democrat	PA-13
Lambert	Democrat	AR-1
Tauzin	Democrat	LA-3
Klug	Republican	WI-2
Upton	Republican	MI-6
Hall	Democrat	TX-4
Hoagland	Democrat	NE-2
Brewster	Democrat	OK-3
Payne	Democrat	VA-5
Jefferson	Democrat	LA-2
Neal	Democrat	MA-2
Kennelly	Democrat	CT-1
Johnson	Republican	CT-6
Levin	Democrat	MI-12

Source: Author's compilation. See Chapter 5.

tion, those most likely to contact members of Congress were whites, married couples, homeowners, those with higher levels of political information, senior citizens, and the more educated. Conversely, blacks, younger citizens, and the poorly educated were less likely to participate. Union households as well as Republicans were also more likely to have communicated with their members of Congress.

Notably, the findings on the behavior of talk radio listeners are dramatic. Talk radio listeners contacted Congress at a rate twice that of the population as a whole (39 to 20 percent). "Dittoheads," as Rush Limbaugh's listeners call themselves, participated at a rate 16 percentage (42 percent to 26 percent) points higher than "non-Dittoheads."

Finally, there is also evidence for recruitment contacts and the effect of a competitive political atmosphere. As Table 6.8 illustrates, respondents residing in districts of targeted members of the House Energy and Commerce Committee and the Ways and Means Committee contacted Congress at a

Table 6.8. *Individual Characteristics and Communicating to Congress*

Higher Than Average Levels of Contacting	Lower Than Average Levels of Contacting
White: 31%	Black: 13%
Over 35: 32%	Age 18–34: 18%
College Grad: 41%	High School Grad: 19%
Union Household: 32%	Nonunion Household: 27%
Male: 29%	Female: 27%
Married: 32%	Nonmarried: 23 %
Homeowner: 32%	Nonhomeowner: 20%
Frequent Church Attendee: 35%	Non–Church Attendee: 25%
High Political Info: 36%	Low Political Info: 17%
Strong Partisan: 32%	Independent: 25%
Talk Radio Listener: 39%	Nonlistener: 20%
Limbaugh Listener: 42%	Nonlistener: 26%
Targeted Congressional District: 35%	Nontargeted Congressional District: 28%

Note: N = 3,800. For codings and question wordings, see Appendix A.
Source: Times-Mirror survey, July 1994.

rate 7 percentage points higher than in nontargeted districts. Again, due to limitations in the survey instrument, I am unable to include direct recruitment in this model.

Examining the effect of these variables with other factors held constant, Table 6.9 presents a summary of the results from a logit model. Once again, I report the coefficients, standard errors, and the statistically significant coefficients transformed into probabilities.

We see that the more educated, whites, those who were married, Republicans, and members of union households were the most likely to contact Congress. Younger voters were less likely to participate. Most notably, with other important correlates of participation held constant in the model, constituents of undecided members of the Ways and Means Committee and the Energy and Commerce Committee were 6 percentage points more likely to contact Congress.

The mobilization power of talk radio and Limbaugh listeners also shines through in the multicausal analysis. Frequent talk radio listeners were 12 percentage points more likely to communicate with Congress. This finding should be treated with caution since listening to talk radio is clearly endoge-

Table 6.9. *Causes of Contacting Congress*

Variable	Coefficient	Standard Error	Partial Effects
White	.48	.12	9
Under 35	−.46	.11	−8
Education	1.42	.14	29
Union Household	.26	.10	4
Male	.09	.08	
Married	.16	.08	3
Homeowner	.09	.10	
High Political Info	.80	.15	14
Strong Partisan	.05	.13	
Republican	.34	.08	6
Efficacy	.11	.08	
Church	.58	.22	8
Talk Radio Listener	.75	.10	12
Limbaugh Listener	.31	.14	5
Targeted Congressional District	.36	.16	6

Notes: N = 3,800. Percentage of cases correctly predicted = 75% (null model = 72%). For codings and question wordings, see Appendix A. *Source:* Times-Mirror survey, July 1994.

nous to participating in politics. Nevertheless, this finding is consistent with other information I happened across on the influence and use of talk radio by political parties and interest groups.

Newt Gingrich's office and the Republican National Committee were especially aggressive about faxing talking points and legislative alerts to various high-profile talk radio hosts during the 103rd Congress. Speaking about a local talk show host, a Congressional staffer told me, "You knew it when he mentioned our number because suddenly the phones would light up right after he went on the air." A Limbaugh producer was even present at the daily meetings of an ad hoc coalition found to oppose the Clinton health care plan. The National Rifle Association (NRA) was especially aggressive about getting its message out over talk radio. Furthermore, although the Democratic Party was a little behind the GOP, both parties now have offices and full-time staff members responsible for tracking talk radio and acting as a liaison to the various talk radio hosts. The Democratic House Caucus even brought in an expert on talk radio to its annual retreat. Although I cannot tackle the topic of talk radio and mass participation in this project, it surely deserves further attention. At minimum, it is more evidence that politics matters and that demographic characteristics alone do not explain participation.

One last way that I test the effect of politics on participation is to take advantage of the fact that the Times-Mirror Poll asked a two-part question on contacting Congress. The first part asked whether a respondent had "ever" contacted Congress and the second asked whether a respondent had contacted Congress in the "last year." Since the information I had on targeted districts was from a recent lobbying campaign (health care), we should not expect living in a targeted state on health care to influence a respondent's previous history of participation. In other words, although the effect of resources and attitudes should stay the same, living in a state targeted for health care lobbying should have no effect on previous patterns of participation. To test this hypothesis, I used the same model as used previously, substituting "contacting Congress ever," for "contacting Congress in the past year" as the dependent variable. As expected, and providing strong confirmatory evidence for my model, living in a targeted state for health care has no effect on having *ever* contacted Congress. The effect for living in a targeted state was .12 with an accompanying standard error of .16.

A Republican Tinge

Finally, in addition to the final legislative outcome – or lack of outcome – evidence from public opinion surveys suggests that critics of the Clinton plan were more successful in their efforts to stimulate opposition to the Clinton plan. As Table 6.10 demonstrates, Republican partisans were more likely than Democrats to contact Congress in 1994.[5] This Republican tinge to the electorate represented a new phenomenon. Comparing those in the Times-Mirror Poll who contacted Congress in the past year with those who contacted Congress in previous years illustrates the Republican bent in 1994 (see Table 6.11).

The results in Table 6.11 are striking. Not only were Republicans and those inclined to vote for Republicans in congressional races more likely than Democrats to contact Congress in 1994, but, as shown by the differences in the past-year versus previous-year measures, the magnitude of the differential was significantly higher than in previous years. In addition, and consistent with this finding, Republicans made up a larger proportion of those who contacted Congress: over half (52 percent) were Republican,

---

[5] The Battleground Poll, taken during the same time period, shows similar results on the partisan composition of those contacting Congress.

Table 6.10. *Contacting Congress and Partisanship*

High Levels of Communicating	Low Levels of Communicating
Republican: 34%	Democrat 23%
Republican Congressional Voter: 33%	Democratic Congressional Voter: 18%
Disapprove of Clinton: 34%	Approve of Clinton: 23%

Notes: N = 3,697. Cells = proportion of groups contacting a member of Congress. For coding, see appendix A.
Source: Times-Mirror survey, July 1994.

Table 6.11. *Proportion of Party Identifiers and Party Voters by Time of Contact*

	Party Identification		Congressional Vote	
	Democrat	Republican	Democrat	Republican
Contacted MOC in past year	23%	34%	24%	33%
Contacted MOC but not in past year	29%	34%	30%	33%

Notes: N = 3,697. Cells = proportion of groups contacting a member of Congress (MOC). For coding, see Appendix A.
Source: Times-Mirror survey, July 1994.

while fewer than four in ten (39 percent) were Democrats. In previous years, the same number of Democrats and Republicans contacted Congress (Democrats composed 47 percent of communicators and Republicans composed 46 percent of communicators).

Using National Election Study (NES) data, Table 6.12 makes this identical point. Although Republicans out-participated Democrats in 1980 (the year of Ronald Reagan's landslide victory over Jimmy Carter and a Republican takeover of the Senate) rates of participation mirrored each other in 1986 and 1990. However, similar to the findings in the Times-Mirror Poll, Republicans in 1994 were more likely to communicate their feelings to their representatives in Congress.

Table 6.12. *Communicating with Congress to Express Opinion on Issues,*
1980–1994

	Republican	Democrat
1980	6.5%	3.8%
1986	7.1%	6.6%
1990	7.1%	6.3%
1994	12%	6.0%

Note: For coding, see Appendix A.
Source: American National Election Studies.

Evidence from two separate surveys not only demonstrates that Republicans were more likely than Democrats to communicate to Congress before the 1994 election, but that the GOP advantage was more pronounced than it had been in past years. While Democratic rates of participation essentially remained steady, GOP rates enjoyed a huge jump.

Chapter Summary

Politics matters: variations in participation and recruitment patterns among the citizenry are the result of systematic political choices by elites. Although more precise information on individual patterns of recruitment and participation is clearly needed, the data reported in this chapter are consistent with the theory of mobilization choices developed in this project and confirm the self-reports of the grass roots lobbyists I interviewed.

As demonstrated in Chapter 5, the legislative targets of grass roots lobbyists were likely to be undecideds, key committee members, and cue givers. Within these targeted states and districts, the survey data indicated more engaged and influential constituents were more likely to be recruited. Those citizens who lived in the districts of legislators who had a high probability of influencing the process – and who themselves had a high probability of influencing that legislator – were more likely to be recruited and to contact Congress.

In addition, the data presented in this chapter provide evidence that recruitment matters and that recruitment choices need to be part of any correctly specified model of mass participation. Any analysis of participation patterns during the fight over health care reform that concentrated only on resources and social-psychological attitudes would have painted an incomplete picture of the causes of participation. The results presented in this chapter demonstrate that the logic of mobilization at the individual level reinforces the biases that exist in who participates.

Finally, this chapter demonstrates that studies that have attempted to look for evidence of interest group behavior at the national level in the battle over health care reform missed an important point. The goal of interest groups was to influence particular segments of the public in particular constituencies. It was to influence particular members of Congress, and in no small way by activating and mobilizing particular segments of their constituencies. The goal was not to move national survey numbers or to convince every member of Congress.

7

Conclusion

> Grass roots mobilization is used for one purpose,
> period – to influence legislative policy. It's not
> about getting more Americans involved. It's not
> about educating people on the issues. It's not about
> making Americans feel good about their political
> system.
>
> > Trade association executive speaking at
> > a workshop on grass roots mobilization

Proportionately, more Americans than ever are exercising their right to lobby and communicate their feelings to their representatives in Congress. Such high levels of citizen participation may conjure up images of ordinary Americans spontaneously organizing to voice their concerns to policy makers. Furthermore, the fact that Americans are writing, calling, telegramming, faxing, and even e-mailing their representatives more than ever might seem like grounds for celebration to those concerned with low rates of electoral participation.

This book, however, has demonstrated that the ringing of phones, the flurry of letters, and the whirring of faxes is not necessarily evidence that Main Street is talking to Washington and that all is well with participatory democracy in the United States. Recent events, such as the National Federation of Independent Business's activity against the employer mandate in the Clinton health care plan, the American Energy Alliance's struggle against the BTU tax, the American Association of Retired Persons' fight against Medicare cuts, and the National Rifle Association's tactics in opposition to the crime bill demonstrate that little about mass participation in the United States is spontaneous. Rather, interest groups and lobbying firms inside the beltway are increasingly utilizing new and sophisticated technologies to water the grass roots outside the beltway.

This apparent growth in both grass roots lobbying and communications to Congress was the inspiration for this project. Working from the premise that a better understanding of lobbying tactics was required in order to gauge the true nature of interest group influence and the quality of representation in the United States, my goal was to understand better the use of grass roots campaigns as a lobbying tactic. In this concluding chapter, I briefly summarize the main findings of the project, discuss their normative implications, and propose some modest reforms.

Results

The logic of grass roots lobbying decisions is rooted in the logic of congressional elections and congressional decision making. More precisely, the informational needs of voters and legislators provide strategic opportunities for lobbyists to influence both electoral and policy battles. Grass roots lobbying is a way for interests groups to provide information to voters and legislators that can influence election outcomes or the fate of a particular piece of legislation.

Given a particular type of information that needs to be communicated, grass roots lobbying decisions are driven by the probability that an individual's communication will influence a given strategic objective. Whether it was an intensive look at one case or a more general examination of lobbying choices across a wide range of issues, interviews with interest group representatives, surveys of the mass public, and my own observations provided evidence consistent with this logic.

As expected, when the objective was a short-term legislative one and the goal was to provide information to legislators about the consequences of their actions, lobbyists were likely to target districts represented by undecided and influential legislators. For example, in the battle over health care reform, the targets were swing members on the House Energy and Commerce Committee, the House Ways and Means Committee, and the Senate Finance Committee. In the fight over NAFTA, attention was focused on the districts of undecided representatives in the House as a whole. In the battle over the BTU tax, attention was focused on members of the Oklahoma congressional delegation who were important and influential members of important and influential committees. Within targeted districts on these as well as other grass roots lobbying campaigns with a legislative objective, lobbyists made great efforts to target those citizens who had the best chance of influencing their members of Congress. Although these constituents were often wealthy or well connected – executives, longtime supporters, and neighbors – credibility occasionally demanded more nontraditional messengers, such as waitresses, Boy Scouts, and senior citizens.

When the goal was a more long-term electoral one and the objective was to provide information to voters and potential challengers, targets were likely to be legislative opponents who were judged to be vulnerable. The Democratic targets for Medicare lobbying in 1995 and 1996 were Republican freshmen who had won by narrow margins in 1994 and who represented a large proportion of elderly constituents. Republican targets in 1994 during debate over the crime bill were members who represented districts that had traditionally gone Republican in presidential races. Furthermore, with an electoral objective, I found that constituent targets were likely to be more broad-based and included those citizens who could most credibly frame the issue.

Whichever the goal, messages were usually crafted to highlight early-order direct costs and mobilization efforts were generally targeted at those citizens most likely to bear early-order costs. When groups had the resources, messages were crafted and tested with focus groups and surveys. Again, with both goals, citizens over whom groups had leverage, citizens who were likely to respond to a request, and citizens who were likely to respond in a way consistent with an interest group's goals were the most likely targets.

Implications

The great majority of the work on mass participation has concentrated on voting. Much of this previous work on mass participation has attempted to explain political activity by personal resources (Verba et al. 1996), partisan attachments (Abramson and Aldrich 1982; Campbell et al. 1960), political interest (Neumann 1986; Verba and Nie 1972), political efficacy (Abramson 1983; Bennet 1986), and political information (Zaller 1992).

Much of the work on lobbying in the past twenty years has concentrated on the relatively narrow area of PAC donations. Also, the debate in the lobbying literature has long revolved around the question of whether groups are more likely to target their friends or their enemies. Different sets of scholars at different times have found evidence and devised rationalizations for why interest groups might want to target supporters (Bauer et al. 1964; Hall and Wayman 1990; Hayes 1981; Mathews 1960; Milbrath 1963; Ziegler 1964), opponents (Austen-Smith and Wright 1994), or undecideds (Ainsworth and Sened 1993; Rothenberg 1992; Smith 1984).

My work suggests that these explanations of mass participation and interest group lobbying are theoretically and descriptively incomplete. What's more, my work suggests that scholars must tackle the two subjects in tandem. Traditional explanations of mass participation find it difficult to explain variations and fluctuations in patterns of participation. This is because they have ignored how the nature of our political system creates incentives for groups to bring into politics particular individuals in particular places at particular times. The ways that politics brings people to participate are far from transitory or unsystematic. They proceed from the very nature of our political system. As my work confirms, resources, attachments, efficacy, and information are certainly a big part of the picture and certainly influence who is recruited to participate in politics. Although findings on the power of mobilization are not novel, this project explains the logic of mobilization and demonstrates the importance of understanding the logic of mobilization if we are to understand the nature of mass participation.

Likewise, the mobilization of constituent communications to Congress must be a part of any model of interest group influence or lobbying. Even more importantly, future work on interest group strategies and tactics must proceed from a proper theoretical understanding of exactly what lobbyists are trying to accomplish. Although previous scholarship has taught us much about how interest groups operate, the lack of a theoretical picture of lobbying and its strategic objectives has limited much of this previous work's explanatory power.

For example, why have some scholars found evidence that groups target friends, while others have found evidence that they target enemies, and yet others have found that undecided legislators are likely to be the targets? The answer is simple. Interest groups do, in fact, sometimes target friends, sometimes target enemies, and sometimes target undecideds. Tactical lobbying choices depend on the lobbying strategy being used and a group's ultimate strategic objective. Lobbyists have multiple motives and have multiple lobbying tools to achieve these motives. Therefore, not only in order to understand tactical mobilization decisions, but in order to study lobbying and interest group influence in general, we need to be precise about what interest groups are trying to achieve.

Lastly, understanding lobbying tactics is also crucial for understanding how issues and incumbent behavior influence congressional elections. Strategic and tactical mobilization decisions and mass participation outside the formal congressional campaign period can tell us much about the nature of congressional campaigns and congressional elections. Scholars of lobbying have paid extensive attention to the congressional electoral connection. It is time for scholars of congressional elections to pay attention to the grass roots lobbying connection.

In sum, looking from the bottom up with survey data and from the top down with data from interest group interviews, the empirical findings in this project demonstrate that requests for political activity matter and that they deserve a place in any correctly specified model of political participation or interest group lobbying. Understanding why individuals participate in politics requires more than an understanding of individual attributes and attitudes. Similarly, understanding how and why interest groups lobby requires that one look beyond financial donations and the direct activities of Washington-based lobbyists.

Pathologies and Reforms

Concern about biases introduced by low rates of mass participation and the supposed power of special interests has created a growth industry for would-be reformers. Although there is no shortage of proposed solutions that claim to have found the silver bullet, my findings demonstrate that because the strategies and tactics of interest groups are imbedded in our politics, reform will not be easy. I have concentrated on only the tactical aspects of one lobbying tool – mobilizing constituent communications to Congress. But my work makes the more general point that reforms need to proceed from a better theoretical understanding of how lobbying works and how participation works.

Interest groups stimulate mass participation because it is an effective way for them to provide information to voters and legislators. The lobbying strategy of mobilizing constituent communications to Congress did not create the need for this information. It did not create the fact that legislators will often base decisions on small, intense minorities, or that legislation with short-term direct costs to an attentive public and long-term general benefits to an inattentive public would be difficult to pass. It did not create the reality that opponents of a policy have the advantage over proponents, or that people react more intensely in opposition to the reduction of an old benefit than they do in favor of a new one. The lobbying strategy of stimulating constituent communications has created none of these realities. It, however, has exacerbated their effects. It has exacerbated already existing forces toward short-term goals and single interests. It has contributed to a society that increasingly finds it difficult to formulate solutions to complex policy questions.

Some might take these findings as evidence that scholars such as Berelson, who were concerned about the dangers of too much mass participation, were correct. To the contrary, the reason why stimulated participation is so effective in conveying information is because participation rates are low. In particular, low rates of participation in congressional elections (only about one-third of the eligible voting-age population typically votes in midterm elections) make legislators particularly sensitive to the information they receive from constituent communications and make them less likely to pay attention to potential constituencies. Similarly, these same low rates of participation make grass roots campaigns with an electoral objective more effective. Narrow constituencies targeted for persuasion can have a large influence in a low-turnout contest.

The usual solution proposed by political scientists for such problems is stronger parties. As a card-carrying political scientist, it is easy enough for me to join the call for more powerful parties that would supposedly mobilize voters and focus legislators on collective results and collective accountability. Nevertheless, despite the discipline's pleas, it is hard to see how parties will become stronger. Short of the creation of responsible party government, however, there are steps that can be taken.

First, interest groups and lobbyists should have to report the money they spend to stimulate constituent communications to Congress. Although a strange alliance ranging from the National Rifle Association to the American Civil Liberties Union rose up in opposition to stricter reporting requirements for those engaging in mobilization activities, the goal is not to restrict a group's right to engage in politics. It is to increase the rights of the rest of us to know who is lobbying. Will such reporting requirements alleviate bias in our system and stop the need to transmit information? No. Given the fact that legislators and voters need information, however, the public should know who is transmitting what information to whom – and how they are doing it.

Second, since low rates of electoral participation exacerbate the effect of information-sending strategies like stimulated communications to Congress, efforts should continue to increase rates of voting. The way to limit the effect of strategies that attempt to convey biased information is to decrease the importance of that information. The empirical jury is still out on reforms like motor-voter and vote-by-mail elections. Scholars need to study these reforms and actively voice their findings to policy makers. Technological advances have spurred the growth in communications to Congress. Careful attention should be paid to new technologies that could increase rates of voting.

Final Words

The central premise of this project has been that elite recruitment of mass participation ties together important questions of mass participation and interest group influence. A theoretical and empirical understanding of the effect and causes of mobilization decisions must be a part of any complete picture of interest group influence or mass participation. The central argument has been that the factors that shape mobilization decisions – and thus the nature of political participation and interest group influence – are rooted in the basic logic of our political system and the strategic needs of interest groups to provide information to citizens and legislators. The theory and empirical analysis presented in this book should hopefully move us toward a better understanding of how groups influence congressional decision making and why individual citizens participate in politics.

Finally, the basic theory of mobilization and participation outlined and the initial empirical findings presented have serious consequences for American democracy. Democratic theories of representation teach us that the legitimacy of representative government relies on the mass public to communicate its beliefs to elite policy makers. Those individuals and groups who do not speak, are not heard – they do not affect the selection of our leaders or the public policy choices they make. Paraphrasing Schattschneider (1960), the logic of mobilization and participation presented in this project demonstrates that the choir leader has an extraordinary amount of power and the accent of the heavenly choir depends heavily on the strategic choices that the choir leader is making.

Appendix A

Sources and Coding for Survey Data

The Battleground Poll

Sample: **National sample of 1,000 registered voters**

Field Date: **August 18–21, 1994**

Communicated with Congress: "Have you called, or sent or faxed a letter to your congressional representative or senator to express your opinion on an issue in the past year?" Coded 1 if yes; 0 if no.

Communicated with Congress about Health Care: "Have you called, or sent or faxed a letter to your Congressional representative or senator to express your opinion specifically on health care legislation in the past year?" Coded 1 if yes; 0 if no.

Mobilization Contact: "From time to time parties and other groups contact people and urge them to phone or fax or call their senator or representative to convey their feelings on an issue. Has anyone contacted you and encouraged you to get in touch with your senator or representative in Washington?" Coded 1 if yes; 0 otherwise.

Sex: By observation: Coded 1 if male; 0 if female.

Race: "What is your race? Are you African-American, white, Asian, or some other?"

White: Coded 1 if white; 0 if anything else.

Marital Status: "What is your current marital status – are you single and never married, married, separated, divorced, or widowed?" Coded 1 if married; 0 if anything else.

Party Identification: "Generally speaking, do you think of yourself as a Republican, a Democrat, an independent or what? (If Republican or Democrat) "Would you call yourself a strong (Republican/Democrat) or not very strong (Republican/Democrat)?" (If independent, other, or no preference) "Do you think of yourself as closer to the Republican or Democratic party?"

Republican: Coded 1 if strong, not strong, or lean Republican; 0 if anything else.

Democrat: Coded 1 if strong, not strong, or lean Democrat; 0 if anything else.

Intensity: Coded 0 if independent or apolitical; .33 if independent leaning toward a party; .67 if a weak partisan; 1 if a strong partisan.

Union Household: "Are you or is any member of your household a member of a labor union or teachers' union?" Coded 1 if yes; 0 if no.

Age: "What is your age, please?"
   Under 35: Coded 1 if under 35; 0 if anything else.
   Over 65: Coded 1 if over 65; 0 if anything else.

Education: "What is the highest level of education you have completed?" Coded 0 if 8 grades or less; .25 if 9–12 grades with no diploma or equivalency; .50 if 12 grades diploma or equivalency; .75 if some college; 1 if college degree.

Class: "Do you consider yourself a member of the upper class, middle class, working class, lower class, or are you not sure?" Coded 1 if upper class; .66 if middle class; .33 if working class; 0 if anything else.

Employed: "Do you currently work outside of the home?" Coded 1 if yes; 0 if no.

Targeted States: Coded 1 if Connecticut, Georgia, Kansas, Louisiana, Montana, Nebraska, New Jersey, North Dakota, Oklahoma, Rhode Island, Tennessee; all other states coded 0.

Times–Mirror Center for the People and the Press New Political Landscape Survey

   Sample: **National sample of 3,800 (voting-age adults)**

   Field Date: **July 12–25, 1994**

Communicated with Congress Ever: "Have you ever called, sent a letter, or faxed a letter to your congressional representative or Senator to express your opinion on an issue?" Coded 1 if yes; 0 if no.

Communicated with Congress In Past Year:[1] *Question wording.* "Have you done so in just the past 12 months?" Coded 1 if yes; 0 if no.

[1] The following is the Times-Mirror Center's methodological note on measuring participation: "The question asked of respondents read as follows: People express their opinions about politics and current events in a number of ways besides voting. I'm going to read you a list of some of these ways. Please just tell me if you have or have not done each at some point in the last 12 months.

Sex: By observation. Coded 1 if male; 0 if female.

Race: "What is your race? Are you African-American, white, Asian, or some other?"

   White: Coded 1 if white; 0 if anything else.

Marital Status: "Are you married, divorced, separated, widowed, or have you never been married?" Coded 1 if married; 0 if anything else.

Party Identification: "In politics today, do you consider yourself a Republican, a Democrat, or independent? (If Republican or Democrat) "Do you consider yourself a strong (Republican/Democrat) or not a strong (Republican/Democrat)?" (If independent, other, or no preference) "As of today do you lean more to the Republican Party or the Democratic party?"

   Republican: Coded 1 if strong, not strong, or lean Republican; 0 if anything else.

   Democrat: Coded 1 if strong, not strong, or lean Democrat; 0 if anything else.

   Party Intensity: Coded 1 if very strong; .5 if not very strong; 0 if independent.

Union Household: "Are you or is your (husband/wife) a member of a labor union?" Coded 1 if yes; 0 if no.

Age: "What is your age?"

   Under 35: Coded 1 if under 35; 0 if anything else.

   Over 65: Coded 1 if over 65; 0 if anything else.

Education: "What is the last grade or class that you completed in school?" Coded 0 if 8 grades or less; .25 if 9–12 grades with no diploma or equivalency; .50 if 12 grades with diploma or equivalency; .75 if some college; 1 if college degree.

"While respondents were repeatedly reminded to think about whether they had done each 'in the last 12 months,' the level of participation reported was extremely high for the time frame asked about. Prior research also has shown that many survey respondents do not have accurate recall about *when* they had actually engaged in a prior behavior.

"Monitoring of interviews also indicated that some respondents were probably likely to err on the side of including some activity (giving themselves credit for something) they had done, even if it was not in the last 12 months. In order to test this theory, and remove the error that results from the social desirability component – where those respondents who had engaged in an activity, but not in the last year said 'yes' to the initial question – the Times-Mirror Center conducted a second survey of participation.

"In the second survey respondents were first asked if they had *ever* done each of the activities. Those saying they had done any activity were then asked to think 'only about the last 12 months, that is since June of 1992,' and to tell interviewers if they had done each activity in that specific time frame. With the social desirability component removed by respondents being able to say they had 'ever' done an activity, the resulting '12 month' figures are significantly lower. We feel the second measure is a much purer and more accurate reading of what people have actually done *in the last year.*"

Homeowner: "Do you own or rent your own home?" 1 if own; 0 if anything else.

Talk Radio: "How often, if ever, do you listen to radio shows that invite listeners to call in to discuss current events, public issues, and politics?" Coded 1 if regularly; .66 if sometimes; .33 if rarely; 0 if never.

Rush Limbaugh: "I'd like to know how often you watch or listen to certain TV and radio programs. As I read each, tell me if you watch or listen regularly, sometimes, hardly ever, or never?" Coded 1 if regularly; .66 if sometimes; .33 if hardly ever; 0 if never.

Efficacy: "Most elected officials care what people like me think." Coded 1 if strongly agree; .75 if not strongly agree. "Most elected officials don't care what people like me think." Coded 0 if strongly agree; .25 if not so strongly agree.

Church Attendance: "Do you go to church, synagogue, or some place of worship?" Coded 1 if every week; .75 if almost every week; .5 if once or twice a month; .25 if a few times a year; 0 if never.

Political Information: Respondents were asked the following three information questions. The information scale is based on the number of correct answers: 1 for 3; .66 for 2; .33 for 1; 0 for O correct answers. "Now I'd like to ask you about some things that have been in the news recently. Not everyone will have heard about them all. Can you tell me the name of the current vice-president of the United States? Do you happen to know which political party has a majority in the U.S. House of Representatives? Can you tell me the name of the President of Russia?"

Targeted Congressional District: Coded 1 if Slattery, KS-2; Cooper, TN-4; Boucher, VA-9; Lehman, CA-19; Schenk, CA-49; Marolies-Mezvinsky, PA-13; Lambert, AR-1; Tauzin, LA-3; Klug, WI-2; Upton, MI-6; Hall, TX-4; Hoagland, NE-2; Brewster, OK-3; Payne, VA-5; Jefferson, LA-2; Neal, MA-2; Kennelly, CT-1, Johnson, CT-6; Levin, MI-12. Otherwise coded 0.

American National Election Study Survey

Sample: 1978 (2,304), 1980 (1,614), 1986 (2,176), 1990 (1,980), 1994 (1,795)

These data are taken from the American National Election Studies Cumulative Data File, 1952–1992, and the 1994 Post Election Survey made available by the Inter-university Consortium for Political and Social Research.

Communicated with Congress: "Have you (or anyone in your family living here) ever contacted Representative [name] or anyone in his or her office?

Was it to express an opinion, seek information, or to seek help on a problem you had?" Coded 1 if yes; 0 if no.

Party Identification: "Generally speaking, do you usually think of yourself as a Republican, a Democrat, an independent, or what?" (If Republican or Democrat) "Would you call yourself a strong (Republican/Democrat) or not very strong (Republican/Democrat)?" (If independent, other, or no preference) "Do you think of yourself as closer to the Republican or Democratic party?"

    Republican: Coded 1 if strong, not strong, or lean Republican; 0 if anything else.

    Democrat: Coded 1 if strong, not strong, or lean Democrat; 0 if anything else.

Appendix B

Interest Group Sampling Frame

Roster of Groups in Sampling Frame

Ad Hoc Coalition of Business for Health Care Reform	Trade Association
AFL-CIO	Union
AETNA	Corporation
AFSCME	Union
Airline Pilots International	Union
Alliance Pharmaceuticals	Corporation
Allied Signal	Corporation
American Association of Retired Persons	Citizens' Group
American Automobile Manufacturers Association	Trade Association
American Bankers Association	Trade Association
American Civil Liberties Union	Citizens' Group
American College of Emergency Physicians	Trade Association
American College of Nurse Midwives	Trade Association
American College of Physicians	Trade Association
American College of Surgeons	Trade Association
American Conservative Union	Citizens' Group
American Council of Life Insurance	Trade Association
American Crop Protection Association	Trade Association
American Dairy Producers	Trade Association
American Dental Association	Trade Association
American Federation of Teachers	Union
American Farm Bureau	Trade Association
American Hospital Association	Trade Association
American Insurance Association	Trade Association
American Legion	Citizens' Group
American Life League	Citizens' Group

American Medical Association	Trade Association
American Nurses Association	Trade Association
American Petroleum Institute	Trade Association
American Postal Workers Union	Union
American Trial Lawyers Association	Trade Association
American Trucking Association	Trade Association
Americans for Democratic Action	Citizens' Group
Anheuser-Busch	Corporation
Anti-Defamation League	Citizens' Group
AT&T	Corporation
Bankcardholders of America	Citizens' Group
Beer Institute	Trade Association
Bell Atlantic	Corporation
Bell South	Corporation
Blue Cross/Blue Shield	Corporation
Boeing	Corporation
Brotherhood of Locomotive Engineers	Union
Brown and Williamson	Corporation
Burger King	Corporation
Burroughs Welcome	Corporation
Cellular Telecommunications Industry Association	Trade Association
Chemical Manufacturers Association	Trade Association
Chem-Nuclear Systems	Trade Association
Chevron	Corporation
Children's Defense Fund	Citizens' Group
Chiropractors	Trade Association
Christian Coalition	Citizens' Group
Chrysler	Corporation
Ciba Pharmaceuticals	Corporation
CIGNA	Corporation
Citizen Action	Citizens' Group
Citizen's Committee for the Right to Keep and Bear Arms	Citizens' Group
Citizens for a Sound Economy	Citizens' Group
Clean Water Action Project	Citizens' Group
Coalition to Stop Gun Violence	Citizens' Group
Common Cause	Citizens' Group
Communications Workers of America	Union
Coors	Corporation
COPE	Union
Democratic National Committee	Citizens' Group

Distilled Spirits Council	Trade Association
Dow Chemical	Corporation
DuPont	Corporation
Eagle Forum	Citizens' Group
Eastman Kodak	Corporation
Edison Electric Institute	Trade Association
Eli Lilly	Corporation
Environmental Defense Fund	Citizens' Group
Exxon	Corporation
Families USA	Citizens' Group
Family Research Council	Citizens' Group
Federation for American Immigration Reform	Citizens' Group
Federation of American Health Systems	Trade Association
Fertilizer Institute	Trade Association
Focus on the Family	Citizens' Group
Food and Commercial Workers Union	Union
Ford	Corporation
General Electric	Corporation
General Motors	Corporation
Glaxo	Corporation
Golden Rule Insurance Company	Corporation
Grocery Manufacturers of America	Trade Association
Group Health Association of American	Trade Association
Gun Owners of America	Citizens' Group
Handgun Control	Citizens' Group
Health Care Reform Project	Citizens' Group
Health Insurance Association of America	Trade Association
Healthcare Leadership Council	Trade Association
Household International	Corporation
Human Rights Campaign Fund	Citizens' Group
IBM	Corporation
Independent Insurance Agents of America	Trade Association
International Brotherhood of Electrical Workers	Union
International Ladies Garment Workers Union	Union
ITT Hartford	Corporation
Izaak Walton League	Citizens' Group
League of Conservation Voters	Citizens' Group
McDonnell Douglas	Corporation
MCI	Corporation
Merck	Corporation
Metropolitan Life	Corporation
Mobil Oil	Corporation

Mortgage Bankers Association of America	Trade Association
Mutual of Omaha	Corporation
NAACP	Citizens' Group
National Gay and Lesbian Task Force	Citizens' Group
National Abortion Rights Action League	Citizens' Group
National Association of Broadcasters	Trade Association
National Association of Health Underwriters	Trade Association
National Association of Home Builders	Trade Association
National Association of Letter Carriers	Union
National Association of Manufacturers	Trade Association
National Association of Wholesalers and Distributors	Trade Association
National Bankers Association	Trade Association
National Coalition to Ban Handguns	Citizens' Group
National Committee to Preserve Social Security and Medicare	Citizens' Group
National Conference of Catholic Bishops	Citizens' Group
National Corn Growers Association	Trade Association
National Cotton Council	Trade Association
National Council of Senior Citizens	Citizens' Group
National Education Association	Union
National Farmers Association	Citizens' Group
National Federation of Independent Businesses	Trade Association
National Grange	Union
National Grocers Association	Trade Association
National Health and Human Services Employers Union	Union
National Milk Producers Federation	Trade Association
National Organization for Women	Citizens' Group
Natural Resources Defense Council	Citizens' Group
National Restaurant Association	Trade Association
National Retail Federation	Trade Association
National Right to Life Committee	Citizens' Group
National Right to Work Committee	Citizens' Group
National Soft Drink Association	Trade Association
National Taxpayers Union	Citizens' Group
Nationwide Insurance Companies	Corporation
Newspaper Guild	Union
Nuclear Energy Institute	Trade Association
NYNEX	Corporation
Pacific Gas and Electric	Corporation
People for the American Way	Citizens' Group

Pfizer	Corporation
Pharmaceutical Manufacturers Association	Trade Association
Phillip Morris	Corporation
Planned Parenthood	Citizens' Group
Procter and Gamble	Corporation
Public Citizen	Citizens' Group
R. J. Reynolds	Corporation
Rainforest Action Network	Citizens' Group
Republican National Committee	Citizens' Group
Schering Plough	Corporation
Service Employees International Union	Union
Sheetmetal Workers Association	Union
Shell Oil	Corporation
Sierra Club	Citizens' Group
Smith Kline Beecham	Corporation
Smokeless Tobacco Council	Trade Association
Sprint	Corporation
Teamsters	Union
Texaco	Corporation
Texas Medical Association	Trade Association
Tobacco Institute	Trade Association
Traveler's Insurance	Corporation
Union Pacific	Corporation
United Airlines	Corporation
United Auto Workers	Union
United Brotherhood of Carpenters and Joiners	Union
United Food and Commercial Workers	Union
United Mineworkers	Union
United Seniors Association	Citizens' Group
United Steelworkers of America	Union
Upjohn	Corporation
US Tobacco	Corporation
U.S. Chamber of Commerce	Trade Association
U.S. English	Citizens' Group
U.S. Feed Grains Council	Trade Association
U.S. PIRG	Citizens' Group
US West	Corporation
Veterans of Foreign Wars	Citizens' Group
Voters for Choice	Citizens' Group
Warner Lambert	Corporation
Wine and Spirits Wholesalers of America	Trade Association

World Wildlife Fund   Citizens' Group
Xerox   Corporation

Interview Schedule

1. Since President Clinton took office, what are some issues for which you used grass roots mobilization to encourage constituents to contact their representative or senator directly?
2. Why did you choose to use a grass roots strategy in the case of _____?
3. Were there specific districts or states that you targeted in your lobbying around _____?
4. In working on _____, how did you choose which districts or states to target?
5. Once you chose which members and districts needed to be targeted for _____, how did you decide whom to mobilize within the district?
6. How did you develop specific mobilization messages for _____?
7. What methods did you use to mobilize?

Appendix C

Chronology of Health Care Reform Legislation

Before examining the strategic and tactical choices of grass roots lobbyists, it is important to understand the basic policy issues, political environment, and chronology of events in the battle over the Clinton plan and health care reform. (For more comprehensive accounts, see Johnson and Broder 1996; *Congressional Quarterly Almanac* 1994; Skocpol 1996; and Clymer et al. 1994.)

The 1,364-page Clinton plan was ambitious. It promised guaranteed coverage for all Americans by 1998. The funding mechanism was an employer mandate that would have required employers to pay 80 percent of their workers' health insurance costs. The plan included spending caps on health insurance premiums, a requirement that drug companies pay rebates to the Medicare program, and a national health board responsible for reviewing prices for new drugs and establishing global budgets to limit the nation's total spending on health care. In addition, the Clinton plan required Americans to purchase their health insurance through large purchasing groups dubbed alliances. The plan also included a seventy-five-cents-a-pack increase in the cigarette tax and a levy on large employers that did not join the health alliances (Pear 1996).

As the Clinton plan was referred to committee there were three other major competing plans. To the left of the Clinton plan was the single-payer proposal introduced by Representative Jim McDermott of Washington State. This plan was patterned after the Canadian system and would have replaced private insurance companies with the federal government. With the single-payer plan the federal government would have collected all premiums and paid all health care providers. To the right of the Clinton plan were separate bills proposed by Representative Jim Cooper of Tennessee and Senator John Chafee of Rhode Island. Neither of these plans included an employer mandate and both aimed to reorganize the health care market rather than introduce new government legislation (*Congressional Quarterly Almanac* 1994, 324).

The following time line, taken from the *Congressional Quarterly Almanac,* charts the chronology of the major events in the battle over health care reform (1994, 321).

January 25, 1993: President Clinton appoints Hillary Rodham Clinton to run the Health Care Reform Task Force.

March 3, 1993: Representative Jim McDermott (D-Washington) introduces a bill to set up a Canadian style single-payer system.

September 22, 1993: President Clinton's speech to Congress introduces the administration's Health Care Reform Bill.

October 6, 1993: Representative Jim Cooper (D-Tennessee) introduces his version of health care reform (Clinton-lite). It does not contain employer mandates. Similar measure is also introduced in Senate by John Breaux of Louisiana.

November 20, 1993: Clinton's health care bill is officially introduced. House leaders refer it to the Education and Labor, Energy and Commerce, and Ways and Means committees.

November 22, 1993: Senator John Chafee (R-Rhode Island) introduces a bill requiring that all Americans have health insurance by 2005 (an individual mandate).

January 25, 1994: In his State of the Union Address, President Clinton threatens to veto any bill without universal coverage.

May 31, 1994: Representative Dan Rostenkowski of Illinois is indicted and resigns as Chairman of House Ways and Means.

June 9, 1994: Senate Labor and Human Resources votes 11–6 along mainly partisan lines to approve a bill modeled on the Clinton plan.

June 23, 1994: House Education and Labor votes out an expanded version of the Clinton bill. To assuage more liberal members, the committee also sends to the floor without recommendation a single-payer plan.

June 28, 1994: House Energy and Commerce committee chairman John Dingell (D-Michigan) notifies leadership that his panel cannot agree on health care.

June 30, 1994: House Ways and Means Committee approves a Clinton style bill 20-18. No votes included all 14 Republicans and 4 Democrats.

July 2, 1994: Senate Finance reports a bill with no employer mandates.

July 29, 1994: A House leadership plan based on Ways and Means bill is unveiled. Employer mandate stays in and Medicare Part C is proposed.

August 2, 1994: The Mitchell plan is unveiled in Senate.

August 11, 1994: A rule to bring crime bill to a floor vote in House fails.

August 26, 1994: Congressional leaders announce that no health care reform bill will be brought up in session.

September 26, 1994: Last-chance compromise bill by mainstream group is withdrawn.

Bibliography

Abramson, Paul. 1983. *Political Attitudes in America.* San Francisco: W. H. Freeman.

Abramson, Paul, and John Aldrich. 1982. "The Decline in Electoral Participation in America." *American Political Science Review* 76:502–521.

Ainsworth, Scott, and Itai Sened. 1993. "The Role of Lobbyists: Entrepreneurs with Two Audiences." *American Journal of Political Science* 37: 834–866.

Aldrich, John. 1993. "Rational Choice and Turnout." *American Journal of Political Science* 37:246–278.

Arnold, R. Douglas. 1990. *The Logic of Congressional Action.* New Haven, Conn.: Yale University Press.

Austen-Smith, David. 1993. "Information and Influence: Lobbying for Votes and Agendas." *American Journal of Political Science* 37:799–833.

Austen-Smith, David, and John Wright. 1994. "Counteractive Lobbying." *American Journal of Political Science* 38:25–44.

Austen-Smith, David, and John Wright. 1996. "Theory and Evidence for Counteractive Lobbying." *American Journal of Political Science* 40:543–564.

Barone, Michael, and Grant Ujifusa. 1993. *Almanac of American Politics, 1994.* Washington, D.C.: National Journal Press.

Barone, Michael, and Grant Ujifusa. 1995. *Almanac of American Politics, 1996. Washington, D.C.: National Journal Press.*

Bauer, Raymond, Ithiel de Sola Pool, and Lewis Dexter. 1964. *American Business and Public Policy.* New York: Atherton Press.

Baumgartner, Frank, and Beth Leech. 1996a. "The Multiple Ambiguities of Counteractive Lobbying." *American Journal of Political Science* 40:521–542.

Baumgartner, Frank, and Beth Leech. 1996b. "Good Theory Deserves Good Data." *American Journal of Political Science* 40:565–572.

Bennett, Earl. 1986. *Apathy in America, 1960–1984: Causes and Consequences of Citizen Political Indifference.* Dobbs Ferry, N.Y.: Transnational Publishers.

Berry, Jeffrery. 1977. *Lobbying for the People.* Princeton, N.J.: Princeton University Press.

Berry, Jeffrey. 1989. *The Interest Group Society.* Glenview, Ill.: Scott Foresman.

Brady, Henry, and Cara Buckley. 1995. "Health Care Reform in the 103rd Congress: A Predictable Failure." *Journal of Health Politics, Policy, and Law* 20 (Summer): 403–410.

Brinkley, Joel. 1993a. "Lobbying Rules of the 1990's Show the Most Vulnerable." *New York Times,* June 16, p. A1.

Brinkley, Joel. 1993b. Cultivating the Grass Roots to Reap Legislative Benefits. *New York Times,* November 1, p. A1.

Browne, William. 1988. *Private Interests, Public Policy, and American Agriculture*. Lawrence: University Press of Kansas.

Browne, William. 1990. "Organized Interests and Their Issue Niches: A Search for Pluralism in the Policy Domain." *Journal of Politics* 52:477–509.

Browne, William. 1995. *Cultivating Congress: Constituents, Issues, and Interests in Agricultural Policymaking*. Lawrence: University Press of Kansas.

Browning, Graeme. 1994. "Zapping the Capitol." *National Journal*, October 22, pp. 2446–2450.

Campbell, Angus, Philip Converse, Warren Miller, and Donald Stokes. 1960. *The American Voter*. New York: Wiley.

Carlson, Peter. 1990. "The Image Makers." *Washington Post Magazine*. February 11, p. W12.

Carney, Eliza Newlin. 1997. "Stealth Bombers." *National Journal*, August 16, pp. 1640–1645.

Chandler, Clay. 1995. "Bellowing for a Balanced Budget." *Washington Post*, September 7, p. B12.

Chong, Dennis. 1991. *Collective Action and the Civil Rights Movement*. Chicago: University of Chicago Press.

Cigler, Allan, and Burdett A. Loomis. 1995. *Interest Group Politics*. Washington, D.C.: Congressional Quarterly Press.

Clymer, Adam. 1993. "Doctors Soften Criticism of Health Care Plan." *New York Times*, October 17, p. A14.

Clymer, Adam, Robert Pear, and Robin Toner. 1994. "For Health Care Time Was a Killer." *New York Times*, August 29, p. A1.

Cohen, Richard. 1992. *Washington at Work*. New York: Macmillan.

Congressional Quarterly Almanac. 1994. Washington, D.C.: Congresional Quarterly Press.

Conway, Margaret. 1991. *Political Participation in the United States*. Washington, D.C.: Congretional Quarterly Press.

Cutright, Phillips. 1963. "Measuring the Impact of Local Party Activity on the General Election Vote." *Public Opinion Quarterly* 27:372–386.

Dexter, Lewis. 1970. "What do Congressmen Hear: The Mail." *Public Opinion Quarterly* 20 (Spring): 523–584.

Dowd, Ann. 1993. "How to Get Things Done in Washington." *Fortune*, August, 9, p. 60.

Downs, Anthony. 1957. *An Economic Theory of Democracy*. New York: Harper Row.

Drew, Christopher, and Michael Hackett. 1992. "More and More Lobbyists Call Shots in DC." *Chicago Tribune*, December 6, p. A1.

Duncan, David Ewing. 1994. "The Triumph of Harry and Louise: How the Mighty Insurance Lobby Skunked Clinton and Demolished His Health-Care Plan." *Los Angeles Times Magazine*, September 11, p. 28.

Fenno, Richard. 1978. *Home Style: House Members in Their Districts*. Boston: Little Brown.

Fenno, Richard. 1973. *Committees in Congress*. Boston: Little Brown.

Fowler, Linda, and Robert McClure. 1989. *Political Ambition: Who Decides to Run for Congress?* New Haven: Yale University Press.

Fowler, Linda, and Ronald Shaiko. 1987. "The Grass Roots Connection: Environmental Activists and Senate Roll Calls." *American Journal of Political Science* 31:484–510.

Frantzich, Stephen. 1986. *Write Your Congressman*. New York: Praeger.

Fritsch, Jane. 1995. "Special Pleaders: The Lobbyists' Art." *New York Times*, March 18, p. A1.

Fritsch, Jane. 1996. "Sometimes Lobbyists Strive to Keep Public in the Dark." *New York Times*, March 18, p. A1.

Gant, Michael, and Norman Luttbeg. 1991. *American Electoral Behavior*. Itasca, Ill.: F. E. Peacock.

Goldstein, Kenneth. 1994. "Mobilization and Participation over Time." Paper presented at the annual meeting of the Midwest Political Science Association, Chicago, April 14–16.

Goldstein, Kenneth. 1995. "Seeding the Grass Roots: Mobilization and Contacting Congress." Paper presented at the annual meeting of the Midwest Political Science Association, Chicago, April 6–8.

Gosnell, Harold. 1927. *Getting out the Vote*. Chicago: University of Chicago Press.

Greider, William. 1992. *Who Will Tell the People*. New York: Simon and Schuster.

Grenzke, Janet. 1989a. "Shopping in the Congressional Supermarket: The Currency Is Complex." *American Journal of Political Science* 33:1–24.

Grenzke, Janet. 1989b. "Candidate Attributes and PAC Contributions." *Western Political Science Quarterly* 42:245–264.

Gugliotta, Guy. 1994. "A Man Who Fertilizes the Grass Roots." *Washington Post*, August 23, p. A10.

Hall, Richard. 1987. "Participation and Purpose in Committee Decision Making." *American Political Science Review* 81:105–127.

Hall, Richard, and Wayman, Frank. 1990. "Buying Time: Moneyed Interests and the Mobilization of Bias in Congressional Committees." *American Political Science Review* 84:797–820.

Hansen, John Mark. 1991. *Gaining Access: Congress and the Farm Lobby*. Chicago: University of Chicago Press.

Harris, John. 1995. "Law Aspiring to Shed Light on Lobbyists Leaves Some Gray Areas." *Washington Post*, December 20, p. A4.

Hayes, Michael. 1981. *Lobbyists and Legislators: A Theory of Political Markets*. New Brunswick, N.J.: Rutgers University Press.

Headen, Susan. 1994. "The Little Lobby That Could." *U.S. News and World Report*, September 12, p. 45.

Healthline. 1993–1994. Alexandria, Va.: American Political Network.

Herring, Pendleton. 1929. *Group Representation before Congress*. Baltimore: Johns Hopkins University Press.

Hosenball, Mark. 1989. "Letters Sealed with Fear: Direct-Mail Moguls and the Catastrophic-Care Bill." *Washington Post*, October 22, p. C1.

Hotline. 1995. Alexandria, Va.: American Political Network. August 23.

Hotline. 1996. Alexandria, Va.: American Political Network. July 12.

Houston, Paul. 1993. "Phone Frenzy in the Capitol – Special Interests Are Using Sophisticated Electronic Networks to Generate an Astonishing Number of Calls to Congress." *Los Angeles Times*, May 16, p. A1.

Iyengar, Shanto, and Donald Kinder. 1987. *News that Matters*. Chicago: University of Chicago Press.

Jacobson, Gary. 1992. *The Politics of Congressional Elections*. New York: Harper Collins Publishers.

Jacobson, Gary, and Samuel Kernell. 1981. *Strategy and Choice in Congressional Elections*. New Haven: Yale University Press.

Jacobson, Gary, and Samuel Kernell. 1990. "National Forces in the 1986 House Elections." *Legislative Studies Quarterly* 15:72–85.

Jamieson, Kathleen Hall. 1994. "The Role of Advertising in the Health Care Reform Debate." University of Pennsylvania press release, July 18.

Jennings, Kent, and Richard Niemi. 1974. *The Political Character of Adolescence: The Influence of Families and Schools*. Princeton, N.J.: Princeton University Press.

Johnson, Haynes, and David Broder. 1996. *The System*. Boston: Little Brown.

Katz, Daniel, and Samuel Eldersveld. 1961. "The Impact of Local Party Activity upon the Electorate." *Public Opinion Quarterly* 25:1–24.

Keller, Bill. "Special-Interest Lobbyists Cultivate the 'Grass Roots' to Influence Capitol Hill." *Congressional Quarterly,* September 12, pp. 1739–1742.

Kernell, Samuel. 1993. *Going Public.* Washington, D.C.: Congressional Quarterly Press.

Kingdon, John. 1989. *Congressmen's Voting Decisions.* Ann Arbor: University of Michigan Press.

Knight, Jerry. 1991. "A Night to Play Let's Make a Deal." *Washington Post,* November 28, p. A1.

Kosterlitz, Julie. 1993. "Health Lobby Pushes Past the Beltway. *National Journal,* April 17, pp. 34–39.

Kramer, Gerald. 1971. "The Effects of Precinct Level Canvassing on Voting Behavior." *Public Opinion Quarterly* 34:560–572.

Krasno, Jonathan, and Donald Green. 1988. "Preempting Quality Challengers in House Elections." *Journal of Politics* 50: 920–936.

Krehbiel, Keith. 1991. *Information and Legislative Organization.* Ann Arbor: University of Michigan Press.

Leech, Beth. 1997. "Conflictual and Cooperative Lobbying Strategies." Paper presented at the annual meeting of the American Political Science Association, Washington, D.C., August 28–31.

Levin, Carl. 1994. "Lobbying Disclosure Conference Report." *Congressional Record-Senate,* October 3, p. S13945.

Lewis, Neil. 1994. "Lobby for Small-Business Owners Puts Big Dent in Health Care Bill." *New York Times,* July 5, p. A1.

Mann, Thomas, and Norman Ornstein. 1994. *Vital Statistics on Congress, 1993–1994.* Washington, D.C.: Congressional Quarterly Press.

Martin, Cathie Jo. 1995. "Stuck in Neutral: Big Business and the Politics of National Health Care Reform." *Journal of Health Politics, Policy, and Law* 20 (Summer): 431–436.

Mathews, Donald. 1960. *U.S. Senators and Their World.* Chapel Hill: University of North Carolina Press.

Mathews, Donald, and James Stimson. 1975. *Yeas and Nays: Normal Decision-Making in the United States House of Representatives.* New York: James Wiley.

Mayhew, David. 1974. *Congress: The Electoral Connection.* New Haven: Yale University Press.

McCarthy, John and Mayer Zald. 1977. "Resource Mobilization and Social Movements." *American Journal of Sociology* 82 (May): 1212–1241.

McDonald, John. 1994. "Health Insurance Money Flows to Lieberman." *Hartford Courant,* June 9, p. A1.

Milbrath, Lester. 1963. *The Washington Lobbyists.* Westport, Conn.: Greenwood Press.

Milbrath, Lester, and M. L. Goel. 1977. *Political Participation: How and Why Do People Get Involved.* Chicago: Rand McNally.

Mintz, John. 1994. "Some Firms Urging Workers to Oppose Health Care Bill." *Washington Post,* August 20, p. A6.

Mitchell, Alison. 1995. "Clinton Applies '94 Lesson to Fight G.O.P. Budget." *New York Times,* October 12, p. A1.

Mitchell, William, and Michael Munger. 1991. "Economic Models of Interest Groups: An Introductory Survey." *American Journal of Political Science* 35:512–546.

Nagel, Jack. 1987. *Participation.* Englewood Cliffs, N.J.: Prentice-Hall.

Newsweek. 1991. "Watering the Grass Roots." May 6, p. 36.

Neumann, W. Russell. 1986. *The Paradox of Mass Politics and Opinion in the American Electorate.* Cambridge, Mass.: Harvard University Press.

Odegard, Peter. 1928. *Pressure Politics: The Story of the Anti-Saloon League.* New York: Columbia University Press.

Olson, Mancur. 1965. *The Logic of Collective Action*. Cambridge, Mass.: Harvard University Press.

Ornstein, Norman, and Shirley Elder. 1978. *Interest Groups, Lobbying and Policymaking*. Washington, D.C.: Congressional Quarterly Press.

Pateman, Carol. 1970. *Participation and Democratic Theory*. Cambridge: Cambridge University Press.

Petracca, Mark. 1992. *The Politics of Interests: Interest Group Politics Transformed*. Boulder, Colo.: Westview Press.

Powell, Bingam. 1986. "American Turnout in Comparative Perspective." *American Political Science Review* 80:17–44.

Riker, William, and Peter Ordeshook. 1968. "A Theory of the Calculus of Voting." *American Political Science Review* 62 (June): 25–42.

Romer, Thomas, and Howard Rosenthal. 1978. "Political Resource Allocation." *Public Choice* 33:27–45.

Rosenau, James. 1974. *Citizenship between Elections: An Inquiry into the Mobilizable American*. New York: Free Press.

Rosenstone, Steven, and Mark Hansen. 1993. *Mobilization, Participation, and Democracy in America*. New York: Macmillan Press.

Rothenberg, Lawrence. 1992. *Linking Citizens to Government*. Cambridge: Cambridge University Press.

Scarlett, Thomas. 1994. "Killing Health Care Reform." *Campaigns and Elections* 15 (October–November): 34–37.

Schattschneider, E. E. 1960. *The Semi-Sovereign People: A Realist's View of Democracy in America*. New York: Holt, Rinehart and Winston.

Schlozman, Kay, and John Tierney. 1983. "More of the Same: Washington Pressure Group Activity in a Decade of Change." *Journal of Politics* 45: 353–373.

Schlozman, Kay, and John Tierney. 1986. *Organized Interests and American Democracy*. New York: Harper and Row.

Seelye, Katharine. 1994. "Hobbling of Lobbying Bill Shows Muscle Power of 'Grass Roots' Conservative Network." *New York Times,* October 7, p. A22.

Skocpol, Theda. 1996. *Boomerang*. New York: W. W. Norton.

Smith, Richard. 1984. "Advocacy Interpretation and Influence in the United States Congress." *American Political Science Review* 78:44–63.

Stone, Peter. 1993. "Green Green Grass." *National Journal* March 27, pp. 754–757.

Stone, Peter. 1994. "Health Care Reform's Price Fight." *National Journal,* August 13, pp. 1923–1924.

Taylor, Paul. 1983. "The Death of Withholding, or How the Bankers Won Big." *Washington Post,* July 31, p. A12.

Thompson, Margaret. 1985. *The Spider Web*. Ithaca, N.Y.: Cornell University Press.

Tierney, John. 1992. "Organized Interests in the Nation's Capitol." In Mark Petracca, ed., *The Politics of Interests: Interest Group Politics Transformed*, pp. 201–20. Boulder, Colo.: Westview Press.

Toner, Robin. 1994. "Harry and Louise and a Guy Named Ben." *New York Times* September 23, p. A8.

Truman, David. 1951. *The Governmental Process*. New York: Alfred Knopf.

Tversky, Amos, and Daniel Kahneman. 1981. "The Framing Decisions and the Psychology of Choice." *Science* 211:453–458.

Verba, Sidney, and Norman Nie. 1972. *Participation in America: Political Democracy and Social Equality*. New York: Harper and Row.

Verba, Sidney, Kay Schlozman, and Henry Brady. 1995a. *Voice and Equality*. Cambridge, Mass.: Harvard University Press.

Verba, Sidney, Kay Schlozman, and Henry Brady. 1995b. "Beyond SES: A Resource Model of Political Participation." *American Political Science Review* 89 (June): 271–294.

Vogel, David. 1989. *Fluctuating Fortunes*. New York: Basic Books.

Walker, Jack. 1991. *Mobilizing Interests in America*. Ann Arbor: University of Michigan Press.

Weisskopf, Michael. 1993. "Lining up Allies in the Health Care Debate." *Washington Post*, October 3, p. A4.

West, Darrell, Diane Heith, and Chris Goodwin. 1995. "Political Advertising and Health Care Reform." Paper presented at the annual meeting of the Midwest Political Science Association, Chicago, April 6–8.

Wielhouwer, Peter, and Brad Lockerbie. 1994. "Party Contacting and Political Participation." *American Journal of Political Science* 38 (February): 211–229.

Wilson, James. 1973. *Political Organization*. New York: Basic Books.

Wittenberg, Ernest and Elisabeth Wittenberg. 1994. *How to Win in Washington*, Cambridge, Mass.,: Blackwell.

Wolfinger, Raymond. 1963. "The Influence of Precinct Work on Voting Behavior." *Public Opinion Quarterly* 27:387–398.

Wolfinger, Raymond, and Steven Rosenstone. 1980. *Who Votes*. New Haven: Yale University Press.

Wolpe, Bruce. 1990. *Lobbying Congress*. Washington, D.C.: Congressional Quarterly Press.

Woodward, Bob. 1996. *The Choice*. New York: Simon and Schuster.

Wright, John. 1985. "PACs, Contributions, and Roll Call: An Organizational Perspective." *American Political Science Review* 79:400–414.

Wright, John. 1990. "Contributions, Lobbying and Committee Voting in the U.S. House of Representatives." *American Political Science Review*. 84:417–438.

1996. *Interest Groups and Congress*. Boston: Allyn and Bacon.

Zaller, John. 1992. *The Nature and Origins of Mass Opinion*. Cambridge: Cambridge University Press.

Zeigler, Harmon. 1964. *Interest Groups in American Society*. Englewood Cliffs, N.J., Prentice-Hall.

Ziegler, Harmon, and Wayne Peak. 1972. *Interest Groups in American Society*. Englewood Cliffs, N.J.: Prentice-Hall.

Zorack, John. 1993. *The Lobbying Handbook*. Washington, D.C.: Professional Lobbying and Consulting Center.

Index

ABC News, 75
ABC News/*Washington Post* poll, 73
abortion, 7, 20, 40, 54, 60
Abramson, Paul, 18
advertising
  newspaper, 1
  radio, 26, 87, 108
  television, 26, 27, 31, 34, 40, 41, 70, 87, 108
Aetna, 104
AFL-CIO, 26, 70
AIDS, 65
Ainsworth, Scott, 127
Aldrich, John, 18, 19
allies, 34, 35, 51, 57, 60, 65, 69, 84, 88
Almanac of American Politics (1994), 80
American Association of Retired Persons (AARP), 68, 85, 125
American Bankers Association (ABA), 1, 3
American Civil Liberties Union (ACLU), 130
American Conservative Union, 79
American Cotton Manufacturers Institute (ACMI), 23
American Energy Alliance, 125
American Federation of State, County, and Municipal Employees, 25
American Federation of Teachers, 82
Americans for Democratic Action (ADA), 79, 80, 90–93, 97–99, 101, 102
Andrews, Michael, 97, 98, 100
Animal Farm, 30
anti-environmentalists, 3
Anti-Saloon League, 22
Archer, Bill, 98
Arnold, R. Douglas, 31, 32, 33, 36, 38, 76
assault weapon ban, 40
Austen-Smith, David, 46, 127

Bailey, Pam, 84

Balanced Budget Amendment, 7, 54, 56
banking industry, 1, 3
Barbour, Haley, 40
Barone, Michael, 80, 89, 90, 97, 101
Battleground Poll, 6, 13, 107–117, 121
Baucus, Max, 101, 102, 103, 108
Bauer, Raymond, 23, 127
Baumgartner, Frank, 46
Bennet, Earl, 18, 127
Bentley Historical Library, 14
Berelson, 129
Berry, Jeffrey, 2, 10
"Big Three" automakers, 2, 65
Bliley, Thomas, 105
Bonior, David, 55
Bonner, Jack, 2, 3, 62, 65
Bonner and Associates, 2
Boren, David, 60, 101, 102, 103, 108
Boucher, Rick, 90, 91, 94, 118
Boy Scouts of America, 3, 65, 126
Bradley, Bill, 101, 102, 103, 108
Brady, Henry, 4, 17–21, 105
Breaux, John, 101–103, 108, 145
Brewster, Bill, 60, 97, 100, 118
Brinkley, Joel, 2, 41
Broder, David, 73–75, 82, 88, 95, 97, 101, 104, 144
Browne, William, 10
Browning, Graeme, 2
BTU tax, 125, 126
Buckley, Cara, 105
budget bill (or Clinton budget), 7, 27, 33, 54, 56, 57, 67, 68, 72
Bunning, Jim, 98
Bush, George, 68, 91, 97

Camp, Dave, 98
Campaign finance, 7, 54
Campaigns and Elections magazine, 25

Campbell, Angus, 18, 127
Cardin, Benjamin, 98
Carney, Eliza Newlin, 27
Carter, Jimmy, 122
Catastrophic Care legislation, 2
CBS News, 75, 88
Chafee, John, 101–103, 108, 144, 145
challenger quality (or quality of challengers), 31, 32, 34, 35, 46, 67
Chong, Dennis, 64
Christian Coalition, 67, 85
Chrysler Corporation, 65
Cigler, Allan, 23
Citizens Action, 26
Citizens for a Sound Economy, 72, 94
Citizens for Reform, 27
Civic Voluntarism Model, 20, 21
civil rights movement, 64
Clean Air Act, 2, 3, 65
Clinton, Bill, 27, 40, 41, 46, 54, 56, 57, 67, 68, 70–83, 85, 86, 88–91, 94, 96, 97, 100, 101, 106, 107, 115, 120–122, 144, 145
Clinton, Hillary Rodham, 72–74, 95, 145
Clymer, Adam, 73, 100, 104, 144
CNBC, 88
CNN, 88
Cohen, Richard, 3
collective action problem, 19
Congressional committees, 47, 59, 78, 79, 84
  House Banking, Finance, and Urban Affairs Committee, 3
  House Democratic Caucus, 12
  House Education and Labor, 78–83, 107, 108, 145
  House Energy and Commerce, 78–82, 89–99, 100, 101, 107, 117–119, 126, 145
  House Rules Committee, 83
  House Ways and Means Committee, 1, 78–82, 89, 96–100, 107, 117–119, 126, 145
Congressional Quarterly Almanac (1994), 83, 90, 101, 104, 144, 145
Congressional Quarterly Weekly Report, 8
Congressional Research Service, 15, 16
Conrad, Kent, 102, 103, 108
constituent communications (or citizens' communications), 5, 6, 14–18, 20, 24, 39, 49, 51, 55, 66, 78, 83, 89, 104, 107, 109–112, 114–116, 118–123, 125, 126
  e-mail, 15, 73, 95, 125
  faxes, 3, 14, 15, 17, 24, 73, 95, 110, 113, 125
  letters, 3, 14, 15, 16, 17, 21, 22, 23, 24, 62, 64, 65, 67, 73, 110, 113, 125
  phone calls (to Congress), 3, 14, 15, 17, 24, 26, 62, 64, 65, 67, 73, 110, 113, 125
  spontaneous communications, 45, 50
  stimulated communications, 1, 2, 4, 7, 8, 10–13, 21, 22, 27, 28, 30, 31, 34, 35, 39, 41–46, 49, 52, 56–61, 63, 65–67, 70, 74–78, 86, 87, 88, 91, 94, 96, 103, 117, 128, 129, 130
  telegrams, 14, 15, 17, 23, 24, 73, 88, 125
constituent intensity, role in legislative decision making, 36–39, 41, 42, 45, 48, 55
content of messages, 42, 43, 44
Contract with America, 57
Converse, Philip, 18, 127
Conway, Margaret, 18
Cook Report, 79
Cooper, Jim, 90, 91, 94, 108, 118, 144, 145
COPE, 12
corporations, 24–26, 40, 54, 63, 66, 75, 76
Coyne, William, 98
Crane, Philip, 98
crime bill, 7, 54, 56, 57, 60, 125, 127, 145
Crossfire, 40
cue givers, 47, 48, 49, 51, 58, 59, 78, 83, 90, 104, 106, 123
Cutright, Phillips, 21

Danforth, John, 101, 102, 103
Daschle, Tom, 12, 102
deficit reduction, 57
Democratic Congressional Campaign Committee, 34
Democratic House Caucus, 120
Democratic Leadership Council, 100, 101
Democratic National Committee, 26, 68, 69
democrats, 1, 2, 6, 11, 12, 27, 31, 34, 47, 56, 57, 60, 68, 74, 79–84, 88–91, 95–97, 101, 103, 104, 107, 110, 112, 120–123, 127, 145
Dexter, Lewis, 23, 127
Dingell, John, 79, 89–91, 95, 96, 105, 145
direct activities, 5, 23, 28, 35, 109, 111, 128
direct costs, 50, 51, 56, 58, 78, 91, 127, 129
direct mail/mailings, 2, 31, 94, 108
district-matching software, 61
Dixon, David, 24
Dole, Robert, 1, 26, 101, 102
Dorgan, Byron, 103, 108
Dowd, Ann, 24, 41

Downs, Anthony, 19
Dukakis, Michael, 70
Dulles Airport, 10
Duncan, David Ewing, 74
DuPont, 86
Durenberger, Dave, 101, 102, 103

Eastman Kodak, 86
Eldersveld, Samuel, 21
electoral (and direct electoral) objective, 4,
    6, 12, 26, 28, 33, 39, 41, 46–49, 53–
    56, 58, 67–71, 76, 77, 91, 97, 126,
    127
electoral connection, 28, 39, 45
environmental regulations, 69
environmentalists, 24–26, 55, 57, 58
Exon, James, 104, 108
express-advocacy, 27

Faris, Jack, 95
Federal Elections Commission, 86
Fenno, Richard, 11, 36, 44
field staff, 31
filibuster, 101, 104
Flaherty, Peter, 27
Foley, Tom, 12, 73, 83
Food and Drug Administration, 65
Ford, Harold, 98
Ford, William, 79, 81
Ford Motor Company, 64, 65
Fortune 500 Companies, 25
Fowler, Linda, 34
Framing
    issues, 39, 40, 41, 43, 45, 77, 86
    messages, 78
    roll call votes, 39
free riders, 19
Freeport McMoran, 12
Furse, Elizabeth, 12

Gallup Organization, 73, 77
Gant, Michael, 20
Gates, Bill, 43
General Motors, 65
Gephardt, Dick, 12, 55, 73, 83
get-out-the-vote (GOTV), 49, 90
Gibbons, Sam, 97, 98
Gingrich, Newt, 26, 40, 57, 120
Goddard, Ben, 87, 88
Goeas, Ed, 6
Goel, M. L., 18
going public strategy, 3, 4, 6, 24
Goldstein, Kenneth, 19, 49, 115
Goodwin, Chris, 77, 84, 88
Gosnell, Harold, 21
Gradison, Bill, 84

Gramm, Phil, 46
Grandy, Fred, 98
grass roots communication, 39–42, 47, 51,
    52, 56
grass roots lobbying/mobilization/campaigns
    (or issue advocacy campaigns), 3–8,
    11–13, 22–25, 27, 28, 30, 31, 34, 40–
    43, 45, 46, 53–57, 59–65, 67–69, 71,
    73, 74, 76–78, 83, 85, 91, 96, 100,
    101, 103–109, 111, 115, 117, 123,
    125, 126, 128, 144
grass tops, *see* key contacts
Grassley, Charles, 102
Green, Donald, 35
Greenberg, Stanley, 57
Guardian Advisory Council (GAC), 87,
    95
Gudermuth, Lori, 6
Gugliotta, Guy, 2

Hall, Ralph, 90, 91, 118
Hall, Richard, 42, 59, 94, 127
Hancock, Mel, 98
Hansen, John Mark, 10
Hansen, Mark, 4, 14, 19, 21, 22, 50, 115
"Harry and Louise" Campaign, 74, 77, 88,
    96, 97
Hart, Philip, 14
Hatch, Orrin, 102
Hatfield, Matt, 103
Hayes, Michael, 127
Hayes, Patrick, 70
Hayes, Ron, 70
Headen, Susan, 74
Headline News, 88
health care reform, 7, 8, 13, 27, 46, 53, 54,
    57, 71, 72–111, 113, 115, 117, 120,
    121, 123–126, 144, 145
Health Care Reform Bill, 145
Health Care Reform Task Force, 145
Health Insurance Association of America
    (HIAA), 73, 74, 84, 88, 96, 97
Healthcare Leadership Council, 84
Healthline, 8
Heith, Diane, 77, 84, 88
Herger, Wally, 98
Herring, Pendleton, 22
Hoagland, Peter, 97, 98, 100, 118
Hotline, 8, 26
Houghton, Amo, 98
Human Rights Campaign Fund, 12
Hyde Amendment, 60

IBM, 86
incentives/benefits to participate, 12, 16,
    18, 19, 27

incumbency, 31, 32, 33, 34, 35, 36, 46, 67, 128
indirect (lobbying) tactics, 24, 32, 34, 35, 109
individual pluralism, 24
information distribution, 39, 58, 65, 67, 76, 83, 126, 129
inside strategies, 3, 46, 60, 74, 104
institutional pluralism, 24
internal group pressure, 64
Isakowitz, Mark, 95

Jackson, Brooks, 88
Jacobs, Andy, Jr., 98
Jacobson, Gary, 31, 34
Jamieson, Kathleen Hall, 77
Jefferson, William, 98, 100, 118
Johnson, Haynes, 73, 74, 82, 95, 97, 101, 104, 144
Johnson, Nancy, 97, 99, 100, 118
Johnston, J. Bennett, Jr., 103, 108

Kahneman, Daniel, 50
Katz, Daniel, 21
Kennedy, Ted, 27, 46, 81–83
Kennelly, Barbara, 99, 100, 118
Kernell, Samuel, 3, 24, 34
Kerrey, Bob, 103, 104, 108
key committee members, 3, 15, 47, 48, 51, 58–60, 72, 73, 78, 84, 85, 89, 95, 96, 97, 104, 106, 107, 115
key contacts (or "grass tops"), 61–64, 70, 87, 88, 106, 123
Kingdon, John, 10, 32, 36, 38, 45, 47, 52
Klug, Scott, 91, 94, 118
Knight, Jerry, 4
Kopetski, Mike, 99
Kosterlitz, Julie, 88
Kramer, Gerald, 21
Kramer, Tony, 25
Krasno, Jonathan, 35
Krehbiel, Keith, 83

Lake, Celinda, 6
Lake Research, 6
Lambert, Blanche, 90, 91, 94, 118
LaRocco, Larry, 12
Lautenberg, Frank, 103, 108
League of Conservation Voters, 12, 25, 26
Leech, Beth, 8, 46
Legislate on-line service, 97, 101
Legislative Demographic Services, 61
legislative objectives, 5, 12, 23, 40, 43, 45–47, 51, 54–56, 58–61, 64, 67, 71, 73, 75, 77, 89, 103, 106, 126
Lehman, Richard, 90, 91, 94, 95, 118
Leo Burnett and Company, 2

Levin, Carl, 14
Levin, Sander, 12, 99, 100, 118
Lewis, John, 99
Lewis, Neil, 73, 74
liability laws, 65
Lieberman, Joseph, 103, 104, 108
Limbaugh, Rush, 88, 118–120
lobbying reform, 7, 13, 54, 129
Lockerbie, Brad, 49
Loomis, Burdett A., 23
Luttbeg, Norman, 20

Magaziner, Ira, 73, 90, 96
mainstream coalition, *see* "rump group"
Mann, Thomas, 16
Margolies-Mezvinsky, Marjorie, 90, 91, 94, 105, 118
Martin, Cathie Jo, 73
Mathews, Donald, 49, 127
Matsui, Robert, 99
Mayhew, David, 36
McClure, Robert, 34
McCrery, Jim, 99
McCurdy, Dave, 60
McDermott, Jim, 99, 100, 144, 145
McDonald, John, 104
McNulty, Michael, 99
meat inspection procedures, 7, 54, 57
Medicaid, 82
Medicare, 2, 7, 26, 33, 54, 57, 66, 68, 69, 70, 82, 125, 127, 144, 145
Mellman-Lazarus-Lake consulting firm, 11, 107
message effectiveness, 71
midnight basketball, 40, 56
Milbrath, Lester, 18, 127
Miller, Warren, 18, 127
Mintz John, 24, 86
Mitchell plan, 145
Mitchell, George, 73, 82, 83, 102
Mobil, 86
mobilization, 3, 6, 8, 11, 12, 20, 21, 22, 25, 28, 30, 33–35, 41–43, 45–47, 49–52, 54–56, 58, 62–68, 72–75, 78, 81–85, 87–91, 96, 104–106, 108–110, 112–117, 123–125, 127, 128, 130, 131
Mobilization, Participation, and Democracy in America, 14
mobilization weight in strategic calculations, 44, 45, 51
Motley, John, 72
motor-voter legislation, 103
Moynihan, Daniel Patrick, 81, 82, 101, 102, 103

NAFTA, 7, 54, 55, 60, 63, 64, 85, 110, 126

Nagel, Jack, 21
National Committee to Preserve Social Security and Medicare, 2
National Education Association, 82
National Election Studies, 6, 16, 17, 21, 22, 122, 123
National Federation of Independent Business (NFIB), 72, 74, 87, 88, 90–99, 101, 102, 125
National Journal, 8, 24, 25, 70, 79
National Restaurant Association, 40, 41, 45
National Rifle Association, 40, 56, 120, 125, 130
Neal, Richard, 99, 100, 118
Neumann, W. Russell, 18, 127
New York Times, 7, 24, 25
Newsweek magazine, 2, 3
Nexis, 25
Nie, Norman, 18
Nunn, Sam, 47, 103, 104, 108
Nuttle, Marc, 88

Odegard, Peter, 22
Olson, Mancur, 19
Ordeshook, Peter, 19
organizational hurdles/resources, 11, 84, 85, 89
organizational maintenance objectives, 55, 75
organized labor, 25, 26, 70, 76
Ornstein, Norman, 16
Orwell, George, 30
outside lobbying/outside tactics (*see also* grass roots lobbying), 3, 4, 5, 24, 28, 38, 59, 60, 76, 77

Packwood, Bob, 101, 102
PACs, 5, 42, 63, 104, 105, 127
Pallone, Frank, 91
paradox of participation, 19
Participation in America, 17
patch-thrus, 66, 88
Payne, L. F., 72, 97, 99, 100, 118
Pear, Robert, 100, 104, 144
persuadability
    constituency targets for, 129
    of legislators, 47, 56, 78, 83, 89, 104
    measure of, 79
petition signing, 21
Pew Center, 116
Philip Hart Papers, 14
phone banks, 3, 31, 66, 73, 109
Pickle, J. J., 97, 99, 100
Plisner, Marty, 75, 88
political demonstrations, 21
Pontius, John, 15, 16
Pool, Ithiel de Sola, 23, 127

pork barrel legislation, 40, 56
Powell, Bingam, 21
Price, David, 12
priming, 40, 56
Project 95, 25
Pryor, David, 102
Public Affairs Council, 8, 25
Public Opinion Strategies, 6, 73

Rangel, Charles, 99
rational choice model, 19, 20, 44, 49
Reagan, Ronald, 1, 122
Reciprocal Trade Act, 23
Republican National Committee, 27, 40, 61, 120
Republicans, 1, 6, 26, 27, 57, 60, 68, 70, 74, 79, 88, 90, 100, 101, 103, 107, 110, 112, 119–123, 127, 145
representation ratios, 115, 116
Riegle, Donald, Jr., 12
Riker, William, 19
Roberts, Cokie, 75
Roberts, Steve, 75
Robertson, Pat, 88
Rockefeller, John, 102
Rockwell, Norman, 85
roll call vote, 5, 32, 39
Romer, Thomas, 47
Roosevelt, James, 2
Roper Center Survey, 17, 21, 22
Rosenstone, Steven, 4, 14, 18, 19, 21, 22, 50, 115
Rosenthal, Howard, 47
Rostenkowski, Dan, 1, 79, 96, 97, 99, 145
Rotary Club, 45
Roth, Bill, 101, 102
Rothenberg, Lawrence, 32, 52, 127
Rowland, Roy, 90, 91
"rump group" (*see also* mainstream coalition), 103, 104, 107

Safire's Political Dictionary, 1
salience of issues, 32, 33, 35, 38, 39, 41, 67, 74
Santorum, Rick, 99
Scarlett, Thomas, 74, 97
Schattschneider, E. E., 131
Schenk, Lynn, 90, 91, 94, 105, 118
Schlozman, Kay, 4, 10, 17–21, 23
Second Amendment, 56
secretary of the Treasury, 1
Securities and Exchange Commission, 62
Senate Finance Committee, 1, 43, 78, 80–82, 89, 101, 103, 107, 108, 126, 145
Senate Labor and Human Resources, 78, 80–83, 107, 145
Sened, Itai, 127

Shaw, E. Clay, Jr., 99
Sierra Club, 26
single-payer health care plan, 82, 100, 144, 145
Skocpol, Theda, 73, 85, 144
Slattery, Jim, 90, 91, 94–96, 108, 118
Smith, Richard, 32, 52, 127
smoking/tobacco, 7, 54, 65
Stark, Fortney, 99
State of the Union Address, 145
Stimson, James, 49
Stokes, Donald, 18, 127
Stone, Peter, 3, 64, 84
strategic lobbying/tactics, 4–6, 10–13, 20–22, 28, 30–32, 42–45, 47, 52–54, 57–59, 73, 77, 84, 105, 126, 128, 129, 131, 144
subcommittees, 24, 84, 95
Sullivan, Laurie, 104
Sundquist, Don, 99
survey sampling, 115
Sweeney, John, 26
Swift-Rosenzweig, Leslie, 25

talk radio, 118–120
targeting, 22, 26, 42, 43, 46, 47, 49–52, 66, 67, 105
    constituent targets, 6, 10, 12, 13, 20, 26, 42–43, 50, 51, 58, 61, 63–65, 69–71, 78, 86–89, 106, 109–121, 126, 127, 129
    legislative targets, 10, 12, 13, 20, 46–48, 56, 59–61, 68, 71, 78, 81–85, 89–91, 94, 96, 97, 100, 101, 103, 104, 107–109, 118, 123, 126, 127
targeting software, 62, 66
Tarrance Group, 6, 107
Tauzin, Billy, 90, 91, 94, 118
tax exempt organizations, 26, 27
taxes, 1, 2, 33, 40, 41, 45, 56, 57, 60, 65, 67, 70, 144
Taylor, Paul, 1, 2
technological changes in lobbying, 23, 24, 66, 67, 125, 130
telecommunications, 7, 54
term limits, 7, 54
third-party targets, 64, 65, 69, 87
Thomas, William, 99
Thomson, Margaret, 22
Tierney, John, 4, 10, 23
Times-Mirror Center for the People and the Press, 116
Times-Mirror Survey, 6, 13, 17, 108, 116, 117, 119–122
Toner, Robin, 72, 74, 100, 104
tort reform, 7, 54, 65

town meetings, 108
traceability, 3, 7, 8, 25, 33, 35, 38, 39, 41, 42, 48, 53, 55, 56, 57, 60, 62, 65, 66, 76, 77, 104
trade associations, 24, 54, 75, 84, 125
Tversky, Amos, 50

U.S. League of Savings, 1
Ujifusa, Grant, 80, 89, 90, 97, 101
undecideds, 47, 58–61, 68, 70, 78, 83–85, 90, 91, 103, 106–108, 115, 123, 126–128
unions, 7, 8, 54, 55, 57, 63, 64, 66, 68, 69, 82, 84, 85, 110, 112–115, 117–120
United States Chamber of Commerce, 66, 73
University of Michigan, 8, 14
Unsoeld, Jolene, 12
Upton, Fred, 91, 94, 118
US News and World Report, 75

Verba, Sidney, 4, 17, 18, 19, 20, 21, 50
Vogel, David, 24
vote-by-mail, 130
voter turnout, 19–21

Walker, Jack, 8, 10
Wall Street Journal, 7
Wallop, Malcolm, 102
Washington, Craig, 105
Washington Post, 7, 24, 25, 75, 88, 96
Washington Representatives, 7
Wayman, Frank, 42, 59, 94, 127
Webster decision, 20
Webster's New World Dictionary, 1
Weisskopf, Michael, 74, 88
West, Darrell, 77, 84, 88
Wielhouwer, Peter, 49
Wittenberg, Elisabeth, 2
Wittenberg, Ernest, 2
Wofford, Harris, 72
Wolfinger, Raymond, 18, 21
Wolpe, Bruce, 2
Woodward, Bob, 57
worker safety regulations, 7, 54, 69, 70
Wright, John, 32, 46, 52, 59, 127

Xerox, 86

Yellowtail, Bill, 27

Zaller, John, 18, 127
Ziegler, Harmon, 127